ROMNEY MARSH
AT WAR

EDWARD CARPENTER

SUTTON PUBLISHING

First published in the United Kingdom in 1999 by
Sutton Publishing Limited · Phoenix Mill
Thrupp · Stroud · Gloucestershire · GL5 2BU

British Library Cataloguing in Publication Data
A catalogue record for this book is available from the British Library

ISBN 0 7509 2235 4

*This book is dedicated to my granddaughter
Olivia Louise Cole.*

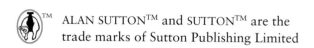 ALAN SUTTON™ and SUTTON™ are the
trade marks of Sutton Publishing Limited

Typeset in 10/13 pt Sabon.
Typesetting and origination by
Sutton Publishing Limited.
Printed in Great Britain by
Ebenezer Baylis, Worcester.

CONTENTS

ACKNOWLEDGEMENTS

For many years I have spent numerous happy hours visiting people and recording their memories of the Second World War; it is only through their help and knowledge that this book has been possible. I am particularly grateful to the late Dick Body, who helped my research and gave me information, advice, encouragement, friendship and hospitality. Tribute should also be paid to Margaret Bird, who makes these books of mine possible through her friendship, very hard work, advice and above all her generosity; and to Harry Cawkell, who certainly improves a rough manuscript by his editorial skills and his dedicated attention to detail. Special thanks also go to my wife Christina and to my family for all their assistance and patience.

I also thank Maurice Addy, Bill Carpenter, Dennis Cole, Jill Cole, George Elvy, Robert Finn, George Frampton, Bob Gearing, Bob Gillham, Patricia Higgins, Tom Standen, Doris Tart, Malcolm Timms and Penelope Tubbs. I must express my appreciation to the following people and organizations for all their help and the loan of photographs, though sadly some of the people have died since this work was begun: J. Adamson, D. Addy, M. and D. Allen, J. Andrews, D. Apps, N. Armstrong, S. Ashdown, M. Ashworth, S. Ashworth, E. Atkinson, D. and D. Balcomb, J. and M. Barnes, J. Bates, P. Bennett, C. Bloomfield, D. Body, P. Body, B. & M. Bourne, B. Brooker, C. Burt, C. Carome, J. Carpenter, J. Catt, B. Chubb, D. and J. Cole, E. and S. Cole, J. and N. Cole, J.E. Cole, A. Coleman, D. Coleman, K. Coleman, D. Couchman, V. Dennis, F. Dicks, J. Elgar-Whinney, J. Ellis, G. and G. Elvy, N. Field, J. Flisher, P. Flisher, Folkestone Library, D. Ford, E. Ford, C. Foreman, A. Franklin, Friends of Lydd, P. Frost, B. Gearing, G. Genders, G. George, B. and J. Gillham, S. Goodsell, A. Hammond, R. Harrington, Hastings Lifeboat Station, A. Holdstock, M. Honey, L. Hopkins, G. Jacobs, A. and S. Jones, D. Jones, F. Jones, M. King, J. Kirkham, J. Knight, M. MacDonald, N. McGhie, D. Marshallsay, D. and M. Mattock, F. Morris, New Romney Fire Brigade, New Romney Town Hall, G. Newton, R. O'Hara, D. Oliver, P. Olver, A. Ovenden, C. Paine, G.T. Paine, S. Paine, T. Paterson, J. Peters, H. and N. Pierce, J.C. Pilcher, J.F. Pilcher, H. Prebble, L. Prebble, S. Prebble, T. Preston, G. Prior, E. and J. Ralph, L. Ramsden, J. Reynolds, A. Roper, S. Sharp, C. Shore, T. Sinden, T. Smart, B. Smith, M. Smith, N. Smith, R. Spencer, E.L. Tart, G. Tart, T.R. Tart, L. Terry, E. Wallace, G. Warren, D. Weaver, M. Weaver, B. Webb, P. Webb, G. Weight, D. Wellstead, R. Wellstead, L. Wilson, P. Winkfield and D. Wythe.

INTRODUCTION

My reason for writing *Romney Marsh at War* was to put on record how the Second World War, with all its triumph and tragedy – and, yes, humour too – affected the lives of those living and working on the Marsh. Also, it is an attempt to try and answer the many questions I am asked about those traumatic times, especially by the younger generation, when I am lecturing on the social history of this unique area. Although primarily written for the people of the Marsh, it is a book I feel should be of equal interest to anyone who served, or whose relatives served, on the Marsh during the period 1939–45, and to all readers with a general interest in that great conflict.

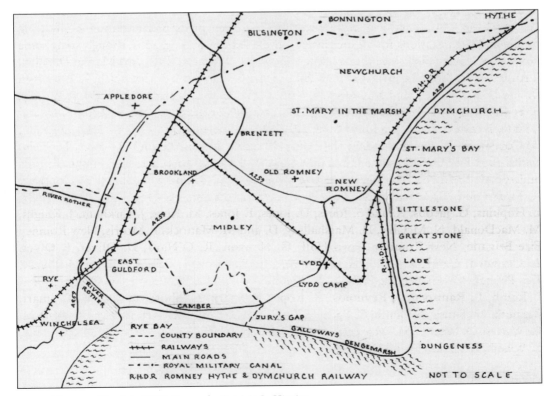

Map of Romney Marsh in 1940. Drawn by Patricia L. Higgins.

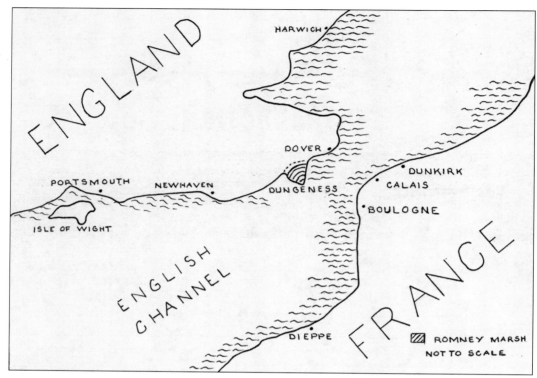

Map of the English Channel. Drawn by Patricia L. Higgins.

For Romney Marsh was in the front line. Its coast was the obvious landing target in 1940 for Hitler's anticipated invasion of Britain, and planned defensive measures included setting fire to the sea, so facing the invaders with a wall of flame, and opening all the sluice gates and flooding the Marsh, thus creating a further barrier of water. Bunkers built for lighting the waves – but fortunately never needed – still exist at Broomhill.

The Marsh coast was also where the first German spies landed, only to be swiftly apprehended; the Marsh skies were where much of the Battle of Britain took place. Its broad acres were where thousands of troops trained, initially for defence, then for D-Day. The PLUTO project – feeding those same troops with petrol through undersea pipelines – was centred on Dungeness. And, finally, for eighty days the Marsh folk endured Hitler's last fling, the destructive Doodlebug.

In writing this book I have had access to the records and logs of the Dungeness Lifeboat Station, HM Coastguard, Lydd Fire Brigade, Royal Observer Corps, ARP (Air Raid Precautions), Civil Defence and local mortuary files. Many Marsh families have kindly searched their attics, cellars and cupboards seeking long-forgotten diaries, notebooks and other war memorabilia. National and regional documents have been studied, where still in existence, as well as copies of wartime newspapers. But the most rewarding task has been to visit, talk with and record the memories of people who personally experienced those

Lydd town viewed from Lydd Camp. Very heavy falls of snow, which began on 16 January 1940, brought a pause in the war with Germany but a battle with the weather began.

harrowing but memorable years. Both in Lydd and the area in general a good relationship was forged between the residents and the huge numbers of the armed and civilian services who shared their hardships. As for the Romney Marsh folk themselves, they witnessed the war firsthand, joined in the battle, endured all its perils and were magnanimous in victory.

Not everyone has agreed about certain incidents, but I have checked the facts as carefully as possible and, hopefully, arrived at the correct conclusions. Unfortunately, space does not allow the inclusion of every story I have been told, however interesting, and I apologize to anyone disappointed on that score. I have, nevertheless, sought to mention in the Acknowledgements all who have helped me, and I trust no one has been overlooked.

A selling centre for promoting the war effort was opened by the local Savings Committee and a shop was acquired in Coronation Square, Lydd. The inhabitants were invited to bring commodities for sale and to purchase savings stamps. As an added attraction, the local population were asked to supply photographs of members of their families serving in HM Forces, as seen here in about 1942.

A Christmas card designed, drawn and printed by a regiment stationed at Lydd during the festive season to send their loved ones at home.

ONE

1938–9

The threat of war with Germany became widely apparent in 1938, and the Munich Crisis on 26 September of that year saw the mobilization of the Romney Marsh Territorials. This force was dispatched to defend Eastchurch Aerodrome, on the Isle of Sheppey – Eastchurch was established in 1909 and was to play a leading role in the Battle of Britain. Dick Body, a Marsh farmer and a sergeant in the Territorials, recalls being sent to Eastchurch on 27 September: 'A local policeman called and said I was to go to our drill hall at Jesson (St Mary's Bay). When I arrived, about 5.30 p.m., I was immediately sent with thirty-four men to Eastchurch to defend the airfield against low-flying aircraft. Our armament was six Lewis guns. Next morning we were required to undergo a medical inspection. Having worked with sheep the previous day I had several nasty sheep-tick bites, as a result of which I was isolated until the medical officer found out what sheep-tick bites were.'

On Thursday 29 September 1938 Neville Chamberlain, Hitler and Mussolini met, and Chamberlain came home waving that notorious piece of paper promising 'Peace in our time'. All Territorials were stood down and Dick Body and his men came back to the Marsh to carry on their normal occupations. But conflict was only postponed and preparations, although slow, were taking place. An air-raid shelter was constructed in New Lane, Lydd, and the population were invited to inspect it on 30 May 1939. A Zeppelin was seen moving along the Marsh coast towards Dover, and David Marshallsay remembers being let out of school to observe this large silver airship. 'Lydd was full of rumours of war, stories of spies and fifth columnists, others were saying the airship was taking photographs of Lydd Camp and making contacts with agents on the ground.' This was not all rumour, for we have since learned from wartime records that the airship was indeed taking photographs, which appeared in German training manuals entrusted to higher officers of the German Forces.

The Fire Brigade Act of 1938 called for the authorities in each area, the district and borough councils, to provide fire cover for their own locality. This became known nationally as the Auxiliary Fire Service. By July the old Volunteer brigades of Camber, Dymchurch and Lydd were obliged to come under the authority of their respective councils, who were 'to provide and arrange an efficient fire service'. New Romney and Brenzett, with no fire service of their own, had enough trained firemen to form Auxiliary Fire Service brigades under their own councils. They were issued with a trailer pump, uniforms, axes and steel helmets, the Brenzett pump being towed by an old London taxi. However, New Romney Auxiliary Fire Service were not satisfied with their lot, stating in a

Looking rather like frogs, Army and civilian workers try out their gas masks at Lydd Camp.

letter to their council that their premises in the New Inn yard had no electricity and left much to be desired. They felt their training was inadequate although they had previously been part of Lydd Volunteer Fire Brigade, where satisfactory training was given. The council recommended that electricity be installed, Lydd be approached about training and that Charlie Carey be appointed chief officer.

On 15 July the first combined exercise in Civil Defence was carried out at Dymchurch, New Romney, Brenzett and Lydd. Imaginary gas and high-explosive shells 'landed' in various parts of villages, and ARP workers, police, firemen and ambulance crews dealt with the 'emergencies'. Also in July 1939 a wireless station was built in Culvers Lane, Lydd, which was manned by naval personnel.

The headteachers of Dymchurch, New Romney and Lydd schools met at New Romney school on 30 August to make arrangements to receive evacuees from the boroughs of London. On 1 September girls from the Prendergast School at Lewisham, with three mistresses, arrived at New Romney; they were billeted on residents in New Romney, Dymchurch and Lydd. With hindsight this evacuation was not such a good idea, but at the time the coast was considered much safer than London, where bombing raids were feared imminent. And who could foresee that the German Army would soon drive the Allied troops out of Europe and stand poised to invade?

'A day of expectation, ready to learn the worst about war with Germany', wrote the young Doris Grimaldi, a Post Office counter assistant at Lydd, in her diary for 2 September.

And learn it she did next morning, Sunday 3 September, when those with wireless sets (radios) tuned in at 11.00 o'clock to hear Prime Minister Neville Chamberlain declare a state of war between Britain and Germany. The next day, 4 September, people gathered at their ARP posts to receive their gas masks and instructions on how to use them. They were also told how to turn an ordinary room into a gas-proof one by sticking brown paper over all outlets and inlets and sealing the floorboards, gas and water pipes and all mouseholes. There were several types of mask on offer: a general service respirator for servicemen, policemen and firemen; a civilian duty one for ARP workers; and the civilian one for the general public. The latter was available in a variety of sizes – large, medium and small – and there was also a large apparatus especially designed for young babies.

Doreen Godfrey, then an eleven-year-old, remembers her experience with her friend Joan Baker: 'We collected our gas masks, then went to a mobile gas chamber which had been set up in the Dolphin Inn yard in Lydd. It was only a caravan really, filled up with smoke. They asked us if our parents were with us; we said "No", but they still let us in. It was dark in there, we were terrified, we couldn't get out fast enough. Both our masks had to be modified: another filter taped onto the mask as the original one could not filter out smoke.' All children had to carry gas masks to school. Mrs Anne Holdstock, a young supply teacher at the time, remembers some, having mislaid their own, turning up with their mothers'. One lady confided to me that she thought her husband looked more handsome when he was wearing his gas mask.

All schools in the Marsh were closed from 5 until 19 September. The Prendergast pupils promptly left the Marsh to join the rest of their school at Sevenoaks. The older children, from the three larger Marsh schools, were told to attend their own village school until further notice in order to avoid travel and to limit numbers. At the larger schools a two-tier system was introduced, so that there were no more than 150 pupils in the building at any one time.

On 20 September many trainloads of troops, mainly Territorials, arrived at Lydd station, either for practice-firing at Lydd Camp or to take up defensive positions in the villages and along the coast. The ATS girls came into Lydd and were billeted in Elm Grove, Cobb Hall and the Commandant's House in Dennes Lane. Maddieson's Holiday Camp at Greatstone and Dymchurch Holiday Camp were requisitioned by the Army. People were hopeful when repairs began to be made

Schoolgirls, left to right: Molly King, Jean Haisell and Margot Baker pose with their gas-mask carriers on their way to school.

to the old brewery at Lydd, but there were sad faces when it was discovered that the building was to be used by the Army.

Motor transport on the Marsh at that time was inadequate for local needs. Mr Bourne of Turks Removal Firm put his new lorry at the disposal of the ARP while continuing to transport the Life-Saving Rocket Apparatus crew from their headquarters in Galloways Road to any part of the coast as required.

Anticipating that Lydd Camp would be on the enemy's list for bombing, a first-aid post was set up outside the camp in the British Legion Hall, with twenty-two beds from New Romney Civil Defence HQ. A second mortuary was also prepared, using the old decontamination building beside Lydd railway station. This had been used initially for fumigating the belongings of scarlet fever victims. The camp was also enclosed by barbed wire – the first time that any sort of fencing had been placed around it since its establishment in 1879. However, although the sirens sounded at intervals, there were few enemy sightings. Ben Tart, an Observer Corps member at Dungeness, recalled: 'After war was declared it remained quiet. We wondered what it was all about. Occasionally Jerry would send over a plane or two, just to let you know he was still there.' One early victim of the war was discovered on 28 September. The body of a British sailor, Stoker J. Burton, was found on the shore at St Mary's Bay, washed overboard from HMS *Kittywake*.

On 6 October all ARP posts were stocked with 500 sandbags, blankets, helmets and gas masks. 'Be Prepared' was the motto. The next day at 2.30 a.m. a large explosion rocked Lydd and the surrounding district when a mine, washed ashore at Dengemarsh the previous day, detonated, wrecking the Coastguard station. The next month Mrs Nellie

Lydd Cinema, on the right, was a popular place with the troops. It opened seven days a week, showing to packed houses.

Prebble notes in her diary that on 4 November the body of a U-boat sailor was washed ashore. On 5 November there were reports of four more German bodies ashore, thought to be from a U15 submarine stranded on the Goodwin Sands. With Police Sgt Tye in attendance, the dead men were taken to the mortuary in Lydd Camp. A few weeks later warning of a peril of a different kind was given on 26 November – local people were advised by the police that Army motor-cyclists were being trained in the area!

The quiet period in 1939 was described as the 'Phoney War', but it was not so peaceful on the Marsh. This was especially so on the coast, where there was the sound of heavy guns during daylight hours at Lydd Camp, troops exercising everywhere, breakaway mines exploding on the beaches and sounds of conflict as convoys passed up and down the Channel. Carefully avoiding the minefields, the Dungeness lifeboat *Charles Cooper Henderson* was launched on 16 November at 5.40 a.m. and stood by the Italian vessel SS *Viloce*, which had grounded close inshore at Lade. She refloated without assistance.

As winter approached, complaints were made that because of the east winds the sirens could not be heard in many areas. On 19 December, more British mines exploded on the coast, five at once at Dungeness, and many properties were damaged. Life on Romney Marsh carried on as normally as possible; people were busy preparing for Christmas. There were organized dances, and the ever-popular concerts where the locals happily displayed their talents. All these events were well attended owing to the numbers of soldiers based locally, to the delight of the local girls. The cinema at Lydd, now granted a Sunday licence, was open every night to packed houses. Generally behaviour was good, the main crimes before the magistrates being for showing lights or riding bicycles without lights. As a seasonal touch, heavy snow began to fall on 28 December.

TWO

JANUARY TO MAY 1940

For Romney Marsh 1940 began with a bang, and then went on to be what is generally agreed nowadays to have been the worst war year. On New Year's Day the Folkestone fishing fleet put to sea, in darkness, to fish the West Bay off Dungeness. A few hours later, at 7.15 a.m., a big explosion was heard both on land and at sea. That afternoon Dungeness fisherman Charles Richardson and his brother Fred sighted some wreckage just offshore, and, with the Dungeness lifeboat Coxswain Doug Oiller, went out to investigate. They found the body of Folkestone fisherman F.O. Weatherhead Jr floating among timbers, boxes, oilskins and a bit of wood bearing the boat registration number F.E.61. The whole crew of that vessel – young Weatherhead, his father F. Weatherhead, W. Ford and R. Cornish – had perished.

Members of the Observer Corps at Brookland, 1940. They, with their colleagues at Dymchurch, Dungeness, Rye Harbour and Hamstreet, played an important part in identifying aircraft. Back row, left to right: Dudley East, Cecil Smith, Joe Sims, Jack Clark, Tim Santer, Bert Jempson, Len Newton; middle row: Walter Smith, Sam Coleman, Mr Wilcocks, Jack Pierce; front row: Ted Solly, Charlie Clark.

Mr Bryant and Ben Tart on duty in the observer post at Dungeness, February 1941. In these early days there was very little protection, even from the weather, but a move to the tower at nearby Spion Kop was a great improvement.

At a Lydd inquest on 3 January Folkestone fisherman W. Hall told coroner Mr F. Flowers: 'It was dark when we set out and we soon lost sight of F.E.61, called *Young Harry*. We heard the explosion but did not attribute it to any mishap at the time.' Mr Hall went on to explain that the mines laid by the Admiralty were on wires, which sometimes broke. Renegade mines were then washed ashore or could become entangled in fishing nets. The Admiralty sank loose ones by gunfire, but if they only punctured the air chamber the mine remained lethal. Coxswain Oiller wished, on behalf of all the fishermen, to protest against these practices. In his opinion the *Young Harry* was sunk by a mine. The coroner recorded a verdict that death was due to war operations. The Admiralty continued to use gunfire to sink mines and other lives were lost.

For purposes of wartime regional administration Romney Marsh came under Tunbridge Wells, with a district commissioner responsible for the welfare of the civilian population and control of all police, fire services and the ARP (later Civil Defence). War Reserve Police – mostly local men – began their duties, and volunteers joined the Special Constabulary, Auxiliary Fire Service and Observer Corps, the latter having stations at Dungeness, Dymchurch, Brookland and Hamstreet, as well as one at Rye Harbour, East Sussex. On 6 January police and the Army were placed on full alert when fisherman's wife Mrs Serena Fair was threatened by an armed man at Dungeness after she refused to give him information about troop movements. Despite a thorough search, the man could not be found. Few restrictions on movement in the area were in force at the time, though on 8 January restrictions of a different nature were imposed: the rationing of meat, bacon, butter and sugar.

A new type of war began on 16 January: a battle against the weather. Heavy falls of snow, with drifts up to 8 ft deep, blocked all main roads across Romney Marsh. Towns

Postwoman Kathleen Twyman delivering mail on horseback when villages were cut off by heavy snow, January 1940.

and villages were cut off for many days, and no trains were able to leave Ashford. With strong coastal gales building up drifts of 12 ft, the situation was even worse at Dungeness and Dengemarsh, the residents ran short of supplies. Farmers suffered losses of livestock, with many sheep, dead from exposure, not being found until a thaw arrived on 29 January. Soldiers under canvas also suffered, with no heating and a shortage of food and water. Many relied on the generous help of residents. One heroine of the freeze was postwoman Miss Kathleen Twyman, who for several days rode her horse Cora from Hythe to Dymchurch with 40 lb of letters strapped to the saddle.

February was an uneventful month apart from gunfire in the Channel and an occasional mine exploding. But strong gales at the beginning of March caused panic at Dungeness when a complete string of mines broke loose. Many came ashore, but fortunately only four exploded, with little damage and no casualties. It was several days before the remainder could be made safe, so allowing the fishermen to work the fishing grounds. On the lighter side, the government urged women to wear lighter-coloured clothing in order to save the darker dyes for service uniforms.

No sirens sounded on 2 April when several German aircraft came in low at Dengemarsh, flew in a wide circle taking in Rye, then across the Marsh to Hythe and out to sea again. A minesweeper in the West Bay opened fire on them, and later in the day a lone plane retaliated with an attack on the vessel, but was driven off. At this time a web of anti-invasion defences was being spun along the coast. Hedgehogs of iron and wooden posts, strung with barbed wire and backed by mines, were driven into the sands and beaches. The seaward side of Lydd was ringed with minefields, the outer side with rolls of barbed wire, concrete tank-traps and pillboxes. There were similar defences at New Romney and Dymchurch, while at Camber large blockhouses (some still there today) were built in the sand dunes.

Five German planes which came into the Marsh via Dungeness on 6 May were fired on by several machine-gun posts, but without result. At least the sirens sounded, though rather late. Nell Prebble recorded in her diary for 10 May: 'Heavy gunfire in the early hours; heard Germany has invaded Holland and Belgium.' While Doris Grimaldi wrote in hers: 'Very busy in the post office; 260 telegrams sent as all soldiers' leave stopped. Chamberlain resigned, Churchill takes his place.' Next day she added: 'All troops are confined to camp. German parachute troops expected. All roads have wire across and are guarded. Five tanks are parked near the police station.' This was one of many alarms, some taken more seriously than others, with tanks placed at the police and railway stations and all roads in and out of the Marsh controlled by the military.

By the end of May the German army had overrun Belgium and Holland and the stage was set for Dunkirk. A tragic naval mistake was the sinking by minesweeper HMS *Lydd* of the British drifter *Comfort* on 29 May, in the darkness and confusion mistaking *Comfort* for the German U-boat *269*, which had just torpedoed the British vessel *Wakefield*.

A controversial incident began to unfold at 1.15 p.m. on 30 May when the Royal National Lifeboat Institution received a request from the Ministry of Shipping to send as many lifeboats as possible to Dover. The RNLI telephoned its eighteen stations between Gorlestone, Norfolk, and Shoreham, Sussex, asking that the boats proceed immediately with full crews, full fuel tanks and towing warps. Hythe lifeboat was first to arrive. The Flag Officer, Dover, told Coxswain Buller Griggs that, with a petty officer in charge, he

HMS Lydd, *a minesweeper of 760 tons, launched in February 1919, took an active part in the war and was present at Dunkirk. She received tremendous support from the people of Lydd.*

would be required to run his lifeboat, the *Viscountess Wakefield*, on to the sands at Dunkirk, load her with troops, and bring them out to waiting ships. Coxswain Griggs pointed out that his lifeboat weighed over 14 tons, and if run ashore she would never get off again without winches. He was prepared to go to Dunkirk but said it would be better to tow three small boats for ferrying troops. Coxswain Griggs reported back to his crew and consulted Coxswain Oiller (Dungeness) and Coxswain Mercer (Walmer), both experienced and decorated lifeboatmen, whose boats were even heavier. The naval officers in charge wanted boats, not advice. And before the lifeboatmen could make a decision the three lifeboats, and all the others as they docked, were commandeered, naval personnel put aboard, and the lifeboat crews sent home.

No lifeboatman had refused to go to Dunkirk. But within three weeks an embarrassed RNLI staged an inquiry at Hythe before a largely naval panel, headed by an admiral, who decided that the Hythe coxswain had induced not only his own crew but also the crews of the Dungeness and Walmer boats to refuse to take their lifeboats to Dunkirk. Coxswain Griggs and his brother Dick, the full-time motor mechanic, were dismissed the service. However, Griggs' prediction proved all too true. Nothing was heard of the *Viscountess Wakefield* for three weeks; then the Admiralty admitted she had been abandoned, aground, at La Panne on 31 May. The *Charles Cooper Henderson* arrived back at Dungeness slightly damaged. Ironically, Coxswain Griggs' advice that the troops should be ferried out by small boats was largely adopted.

Invasion seemed imminent. The organization of Britain's scantily armed forces to repel the Germans fell to Gen Sir Edmund Ironside. He gave the task of defending the coast from Sheppey (Kent) to Rye (East Sussex) to the 1st London Division, whose armaments consisted of only eleven 25-pounder field guns, no anti-tank guns and a mere twenty-one Bren-gun carriers. The Observer Corps at Dungeness had only rifles and five rounds of ammunition each. Ben Tart recalls: 'We were told "as long as you get one German with the five rounds that will be OK". We had no training for guns; the only experience I had of firing guns was at the fair. Two or three of the older men had been in the First World War. Old Oliver Haines, he was in the trenches, so he could handle a gun all right. He used to say "If the buggers land here I shan't have one, I'll have two or three".'

As the threats of invasion increased the War Minister, Mr Anthony Eden, broadcast for men to join the Local Defence Volunteers, and the men of the Marsh stepped forward willingly. Platoons were set up in Lydd, Dymchurch, New Romney and Brenzett. In July they became the Home Guard – armed largely with shotguns, some antique weapons and one First World War machine-gun (without ammunition), which had been presented to one of the towns and in whose town hall I believe it still reposes today.

THREE

JUNE AND JULY 1940

As the year progressed enemy activity intensified, with the prelude to the Battle of Britain ebbing and flowing in the sky above Romney Marsh. So far, on the ground, little notice had been taken of the air-raid sirens, which often proved to be false alarms. Now the dangers could be seen and heard; workers in the field became more wary, while schoolchildren were more promptly shepherded to shelter. Checks, too, were made when the children arrived at school to see that they had their gas masks.

With the very real threat of invasion, there was much discussion about evacuation of the Marsh, the first talks concerning 'Romney' sheep. It was decided they should be moved to the West Country, and an order was given to the shearing gangs – and in particular to Fred Apps of Brookland, who employed the largest gangs – that contrary to usual custom all sheep on the Marsh should be shorn before those on the neighbouring hills; at least the Germans would not get the wool. In total 65,000 Romneys were purchased by the government, marked with a broad arrow on their backs and transported westward. This was all prepared before any plan was made to ensure the safety of the women and children.

On the 'Careless Talk Costs Lives' front a warning was issued by the Ministry of Information to vicars and editors of church and parish magazines in each diocese:

Don't mention casualties resulting from air raids or any other cause in case they occur near some vital point.

Don't say that the path through the churchyard or road to the west door cannot be used as it is blocked by a machine-gun point.

Don't advertise that the parish hall or the tennis club is being occupied by troops.

Don't say that the regiments are now attending church services or socials.

Don't say that the LDVs have established a machine-gun post beside the fairway to the 8th hole.

Don't gossip about such things if you have not seen them published before.

In consequence, Marsh magazines of the period offer little information about the war.

Although civilian access to the coast and other parts of the Marsh was restricted, the young lads too old to be evacuated took scant notice, cycling out to investigate any incident that occurred and often getting there before the police or the Army. Most kept maps and one of the few that have survived was kept by young Robert Finn. For 1940 it shows: pom-pom guns around Rye radar station at Brookland, built in 1939; four blockhouses close to the sea wall at Jury's Gap; two 9-inch guns on Dungeness Point; a searchlight unit near the lifeboat house at Dungeness; a sentry post on the Post Office cross-Channel telephone cables at Dungeness; four blockhouses between Dungeness and Littlestone; a road block and sentry post beside Maddieson's Holiday Camp at Greatstone; naval guns on Littlestone golf course; more searchlight units at St Mary's Bay and Dymchurch; blockhouses near the Star Inn and at Honeychild Manor at St Mary-in-the-Marsh; many blockhouses around New Romney and Lydd; five field guns at Old Romney; a searchlight unit at Bluehouse Farm, Brenzett; a barbed wire entanglement and road block at the Marsh entrance to Appledore; and blockhouses lining the whole length of the Royal Military Canal on its inland side.

Although the Battle of Britain officially took place between 8 August and 31 October, the air battles actually started at the beginning of June and became bigger and fiercer throughout July. On 1 June a Spitfire was shot down near the water tower on Dengemarsh. The pilot was unhurt and his aircraft was recovered. The Civil Defence reported two more Spitfires down near Jesson (St Mary's Bay). On 9 June a large number of British planes crossed the Marsh in formation, heading for France, where on calm, clear nights one could hear explosions and see the glow of fires. On 18 June a skirmish over Dengemarsh and Lydd between three Spitfires and three Messerschmitts ended in the Spitfires chasing the enemy planes towards New Romney and out to sea off Littlestone.

In the early hours of 20 June there was heavy gunfire in the Channel and Ben Tart, a member of the Observer Corps who was on duty at Dungeness, recalls: 'We saw this ship –

The SS Roseburn *beached at Dengemarsh after being attacked by a torpedo boat, 20 June 1940.*

Sands Estate, Dymchurch, 1940. Several small road bridges across the dykes (which conveyed surface water to the sea) were destroyed to make it difficult for an invading army.

we know now it was the SS *Roseburn* – coming up. She was not in convoy and it was light as day, a full moon. She was a mile or two off the Point, and almost immediately we could hear, before we saw, the torpedo boat. He came up behind the *Roseburn* right under the rays of the moon; you could see the silhouette of the *Roseburn*. At first he fired many tracers, but she kept going, and the next thing she went up with a huge bang, and Jerry turned round and went off as fast as he could go.'

This attack was also witnessed from the Royal Naval Shore Signal Station at Dungeness and the lifeboat was called out. Coxswain Doug Oiller wrote in his log:

At 2.55 a.m. on 20 June I received a message from RNSSS Dungeness. I at once called crew and helpers, launched as quickly as possible. We proceeded to the position and found the steamer *Roseburn* sinking slowly for'ard and part of her crew were in boats. We transferred them and their luggage to the lifeboat. I then went on board to see the captain. I told him he had better beach his vessel and arrange a tug. He told me a boat with his crew were missing. I dispatched at once the lifeboat, but a naval drifter had picked them up and was going to Dover. The lifeboat returned to station with the ship's crew. On returning we stood by and waited for the tug. It tried towing, but after 1½ hours we had to give up and beached her at Dengemarsh. We remained alongside, then returned to station with crew and an injured man at 1.30 p.m.

After the war the *Roseburn* was blown up as a danger to shipping.

A week later, on 27 June, Sgt McQueen, flying a Hurricane, ditched in the sea following a dogfight. Doug Oiller and a scratch crew – for most of the regulars were away fishing –

This blown-up bridge led to the Tudor Estate, Dymchurch, 1940.

were guided to the area by two RAF planes. But although one of the crew went overboard to put a rope round the pilot, attempts to resuscitate him failed.

To strengthen the coast garrison the Queen's Regiment was drafted in and at once began building gunpits at Dengemarsh and Dungeness, while the Royal Engineers laid hundreds of landmines. At this time mines were laid too close to the lifeboat house, presenting a danger at every launch. The Army and Navy were at loggerheads about who was in charge of the area. Eventually, the Navy came out on top and the Royal Engineers were ordered to remove the offending mines. As their exact positions were uncharted it was decided to find and detonate them one at a time. As the first one went up so did fifty more, the blast lifting the roof off the lifeboat house, shattering many windows at Dungeness and killing lots of fish.

The Army then decided the lifeboat house would make a good machine-gun post, so they entangled it in barbed wire and laid more mines. Once again the Navy had to insist that the lifeboat be free to launch. As piggy-in-the-middle it was a difficult time for the lifeboatmen. No longer could they launch on the coxswain's say-so. No matter what the circumstances permission had to be given by the Admiralty, Dover. And although it was the Navy's job to inform naval shipping and the Army when the lifeboat was afloat, there was always the fear of being mistaken for an enemy vessel. Despite all this, the crew never failed to answer a call.

On 1 July King George VI visited the Marsh to inspect the coastal defences, accompanied by Winston Churchill, Gen Smuts and Gen Pile, GOC Anti-aircraft Command. Gen Pile had served at Lydd Camp in command of the 3rd Royal Tank

A Hurricane being recovered from the shingle beach at Dengemarsh after a forced landing, 17 July 1940.

Regiment in 1928. Although the royal visit was 'secret', the local grapevine excelled itself: as the King passed through Lydd many people lined the Ness road and children were hurriedly brought from school to cheer him and his party. Twice the sirens sounded as German planes came in high, flew inland and then returned to cross the coast between Camber and Rye. On both occasions the anti-aircraft guns opened fire on them.

On 10 July at 1.15 p.m., after an air battle over the Marsh, three planes were seen to crash into the sea 4 miles off Lade. The Dungeness lifeboat was launched at 1.30 p.m. Only wreckage was found. One of the planes was a Hurricane which had collided with a Dornier. The pilot, Flg Off T.P.K. Higgs, baled out but was killed, his body being washed ashore sometime later at Noordwijk, Holland. The Dornier came down near the Dungeness Buoy. Two of its crew, Fw Umpkelmann and Fm Osovsky, lost their lives, but the remaining two, Hptm Krieger and Ofw Werner Thalman, both injured, were picked up by a naval speedboat. The third plane, a Messerschmitt Me110, was shot down. Both its pilot, Ltn Kishrich, and his crewman were killed.

With air battles and anti-aircraft fire increasing in intensity it was becoming risky to be caught out in the open without a steel helmet. It was therefore agreed that the general public could take cover in the newly constructed air-raid shelters at the five Marsh schools. Most Marsh people joined some kind of civilian organization – St John Ambulance, ARP, etc. – to aid the war effort.

There are still many reminders of the war. This blockhouse on the bank of the Royal Military Canal at Appledore was used to guard the bridge linking the Marsh to the high ground, and is seen here in 1995.

Meanwhile, the local courts dealt mainly with such crimes as showing a light after dark. ARP wardens really did dash around shouting 'Put that light out', for even a small light in a blacked-out area could be seen by an enemy aircraft from a great height. The fine for a light offence was usually 10s, a considerable fee in those days. Failing to immobilize a vehicle cost even more – as much as £2.

The air warfare continued. On 17 July a Hurricane made a forced landing on the beach at Dengemarsh. The pilot, Flg Off Humpherson, was unhurt and his plane was successfully recovered. On the same day bombs fell on farmland at Brookland, making huge craters. A 25-year-old German airman, Wellin Gurfons, was killed at Newchurch when his parachute failed to open. On 25 July, Dungeness lifeboatmen were called out in the late afternoon to rescue the crew of a steamship sinking off Sandgate; it was one of a convoy that had been attacked by sixty dive-bombers with the loss of five ships and damage to several others. The Dover lifeboat had already rescued the crew, but Coxswain Oiller decided to escort the convoy as far as Dungeness, where the lifeboat berthed at 7.00 p.m. At the same time troops manning the searchlight battery at Dengemarsh were machine-gunned by a German plane which circled over them several times. No one was injured.

At the end of July two more ships were lost in attacks on convoys, but the RAF shot down thirty-five enemy planes in dogfights over the Channel. On 29 July Lydd was the

WARNING

Coastal Districts of Romney Marsh, Lydd and New Romney

Under **DEFENCE REGULATION** No. 38a, any stealing or scrounging from evacuated houses or damaged premises in these areas renders the offender liable to be charged with the crime of

LOOTING

and subject, on conviction, to be sentenced to

PENAL SERVITUDE OR DEATH

As more properties became damaged through enemy action, this poster was displayed to warn would-be looters of the penalties they faced if caught.

target of a raid, but anti-aircraft fire managed to keep the bombers at bay and they eventually dropped their bombs on farmland to the west and north. On 30 July the Duke of Gloucester visited Lydd to inspect the troops in the camp. It was also the day that Lydd telephone exchange became automatic, the first one in the locality to do so. Area telephone engineer Jack Bayley was carrying out such vital war work that he had an armed escort wherever he went.

FOUR

SPIES!!

By the end of June 1940 the German Army had swept west through Europe and Hitler contemplated the invasion of the British Isles under the code name Operation Sealion. In September 1940 his plans for such an act were issued. The army was to land strong forces in southern England, with the co-operation of their navy and airforce, and to defeat the British forces and occupy London. Other areas of England would be taken over as opportunities presented themselves. The 16th and 9th German armies, as Army Group A, were to be entrusted with this task. The first objective was to occupy the south coast between Folkestone and Worthing and then form a bridgehead 20 to 30 km deep. Fortunately, this never materialized, but in 1940 it was a very real threat.

Obviously the Germans were anxious to know what opposition they might encounter. But if the two pairs of spies caught on the Marsh coast on 3 and 4 September 1940 were anything to judge their effectiveness by, their spy network was amateurish to say the least. José Rudolph Waldberg and Carl Henrich Meir were caught at Dungeness. Waldberg, born in Mainz, Germany, of a German father and a French mother, joined the German espionage service in 1938 and was trained as a spy at Wiesbaden. His assignment on coming to Britain was to assess the military presence and strength and the positions of the fortifications and types of guns. Meir, born in Coblenz in 1916, was of Dutch nationality, but after he was captured it was discovered that he had a passport issued to him at Innsbruck in November 1938. His task was to monitor troop movements, listen to information and try to locate the positions of airfields.

The other two spies were Charles Van der Kieboom and Sjoerd Pons. Kieboom had been born in Japan to a Japanese mother and a Dutch father. He carried a passport issued to him in Amsterdam in 1938. Pons, a Dutch subject born in Amsterdam in 1912, was a friend of Kieboom and was involved with him in criminal activities before the Second World War. Pons could speak very little English and stated at his trial that he had planned to give himself up as soon as he set foot on English soil.

The German espionage service had selected these four, given them very brief training and then taken them to Boulogne. On 2 September 1940 they were given a farewell party at Le Touquet. They were then put aboard a fishing cutter which took them to a position 3 miles off Boulogne, where they were joined by two German minesweepers, their escorts across the Channel. When they came to a position about 5 miles off Dungeness the minesweepers departed. The cutter continued until she was about a mile off the English coast. Waldberg and Meir were placed in one dinghy and Kieboom and Pons in another. Each pair was given a case that contained a wireless and some clothing, and a sack packed with provisions and two small spades. Kieboom and Pons came ashore between West Hythe and Dymchurch in the early hours. They decided that one of them should proceed inland to check for troops. As soon as Kieboom made the sea wall he was challenged by Pte Tollervey, serving with the Somerset Light Infantry. Kieboom told the soldier he was a Dutch refugee, but when he was searched later by an officer he was found to have a loaded revolver and was arrested. Just 30 minutes later Pons was also seen and challenged and he, too, was arrested. Their wireless and provisions were discovered a short time later in the corner of a field. To be captured within an hour of landing on British soil does not seem very professional or what one might have expected from a German espionage unit.

Waldberg and Meir came ashore at Dungeness. At his trial Meir stated that just before they beached they thought they had observed a small vessel approaching them and in panic Waldberg threw overboard his pistol, secret code and maps, not wishing to be found with incriminating evidence. However, no boat was ever traced. Once beached they hid their belongings under a lifeboat washed ashore from the Southern Railway steamer *Normannia*, lost at Dunkirk some months earlier. At first light they moved inland a short distance and hid in a very large holly bush, of the type which can be seen on the Holmstone today. When they became thirsty it was decided that Meir should walk to the nearest village for drink and cigarettes. He entered Lydd, walking down Ness Road until he came to the Rising Sun public house. Although it was only 9.30 a.m., the door was open to allow the newly

scrubbed steps to dry. Mrs Mabel Cole, the landlady, was most surprised when a tall man dressed like a seaman in black jacket, trousers and a fisherman's jumper came into her bar, asked for food and then for a champagne cider. This had long been a discontinued line but was advertised on the wall outside. She explained that the premises were not open yet but if he came back later she would serve him. Meir went out and she saw him pacing up and down, which made her suspicious enough to ring her husband Cliff, a local butcher. When Meir returned to the Rising Sun he was served with a glass of cider, and after a short conversation with Mr Cole he departed. As he went out of the door two men entered. Meir said 'Good day, gentlemen'. One of these men was Rennie Mansfield, an inspector of the Aeronautical Inspection Directorate attached to Shorts at Rochester. Mrs Cole told Rennie of her suspicions, saying 'I never had any doubt that he was a spy.'

Mrs Wallace, the widow of the late Mr Mansfield, remembers the incident well today:

Mabel Cole, whose suspicions led to the arrest of German spies who had landed at Dungeness, with her husband Cliff and daughter Doris.

Rennie came back to the house and told me of his suspicions and said that he was going to challenge him. I said 'You can't'. He said he would use his AID pass as it looked official. Rennie was an aircraft inspector and he had his pass and photograph on him. He went off in the car towards Dungeness, taking the dog with him. He later told me that he caught up with the man and got out of the car to speak to him. He told the man that it was a prohibited area and that no unauthorized person was allowed there, and could he see his papers. The man asked what authority he had for his enquiries, and Rennie produced his AID card and waved it in front of the man, saying 'I am responsible for the security of this area.' The man said he was a Dutch refugee. Rennie was rather unsure about the man's answer, but asked him to get into the car, which he did with no hesitation. Rennie took him to the police station where Sergeant Tye was.

Sgt Joe Tye (on the right) and PC Jack Carpenter at Lydd Police Station in 1940.

Sgt Tye had already received two telephone calls and someone had alerted PC P. Flisher, who was in Coronation Square. Sgt Tye questioned Meir, who replied 'I am a Dutch subject. I have landed on the beach in a boat. I came from France. I have left a sack of food in a boat on the beach, and if you like I will show it to you.' Sgt Tye, with PCs Cooper and Carpenter, escorted Meir to Dungeness, where he had hidden his belongings. In all this time Meir never said anything about the presence of Waldberg, but Sergeant Tye naturally had been alerted about the two spies caught at Dymchurch and thought that there was possibly a second spy at Dungeness. One of his constables, PC Fred Jones, was a wildfowler and very familiar with Dungeness, so Sgt Tye asked him to change into civilian clothes and have a wander around with his shotgun. Although PC Jones stayed out all night, he saw and heard nothing.

The next day Sgt Tye deployed most of his constables in the Dungeness area and soon one of them noticed a man walking along the beach. He shouted to him and alerted Sgt Tye, who went over to the man and asked him where he was going. He replied in French. Sgt Tye asked him 'Coucher?', meaning 'Where did you sleep?' The man pointed towards one of the large holly bushes about 400 yd from the Lydd–Dungeness road. The policemen searched the tree and in one of its forks two cases were found, one containing five batteries and the other the transmitter set and a Morse key. There were also two suitcases and a raincoat and an aerial running from one bush to another. Sgt Tye arrested the man and the constables gathered all the equipment and returned to Lydd police station, where the man was detained. Mr George Bunston, a local fisherman, had already discovered some German equipment under a fisherman's dinghy and handed it over to the police.

In November 1940 all four spies were tried at the Old Bailey. It was revealed during the trial that Waldberg had already transmitted some messages in French: 'Arrived safely. Document destroyed, English patrol 200 metres from coast beach with brown net and railway sleepers at a distance of 15 metres. No mines, few soldiers, unfinished blockhouse,

Sgt Tye points out the holly bush where spy José Rudolph Waldberg hid and transmitted messages to France before being caught. This photograph was taken in 1957 after Sgt Tye had retired from the police force.

new road, Waldberg.' Another communication read 'Meir prisoner, English police searching for me, am cornered, situation difficult, I can resist thirst until Saturday if I am to resist, send aeroplanes Wednesday evening, 11 o'clock 3 kilometres north of point. Arrival, long live Germany, Waldberg.' A further message read 'This is the exact position yesterday evening six o'clock. Three Messerschmitts fired machine gun in my direction, 300 metres south of water tower painted red. Prisoner. Long live Germany.'

There wasn't much in any of their defences; they had been caught red-handed. Kieboom, Waldberg and Meir were found guilty and sentenced to death. Pons, for some unknown reason, was reprieved. Possibly it was thought that he was of more use as a double agent. In total about thirty spies were caught in the British Isles during the war, including the Marsh four.

FIVE

AUGUST AND SEPTEMBER 1940

Probably due to low cloud, the first week of August brought welcome respite from air raids. 'A peaceful lull at last', one of our diarists noted. It gave the farmers a chance to gather the harvest without constant enemy interruption and enabled the coastal defences to be strengthened with a series of blockhouses and gunpits being constructed to the north of Camber, stretching to the north of Lydd. The troops, it was observed, were working with more enthusiasm, perhaps because the government had just given them sixpence more per day.

On 3 August, at a special meeting at New Romney presided over by its town clerk and attended by Kent's director of education, Mr P.R. Morris, the head teachers of Dymchurch, Dungeness, New Romney and Lydd were briefed on arrangements to evacuate their schoolchildren. In turn they held meetings to explain the arrangements to the parents. All schools were closed at 3.30 p.m. on 8 August and two days later the evacuation began, as a correspondent from a local paper aboard one of the evacuation coaches reported:

The large blockhouse that still stands sentinel over the sand dunes at Camber, 1995.

On 10 August 112 children of Lydd Council school, 46 from New Romney and 16 from Dungeness were evacuated to Haywards Heath. They travelled with their teachers and voluntary helpers in six motor coaches. The weather was perfect and the children were in high spirits. At Lydd the children were seen off by the mayor, Alderman G.T. Paine, who wished them a pleasant and safe journey, and he said he hoped to welcome them all home in the near future. All infants were given a doll or teddy bear to amuse them on their way. There were no tears; on the contrary the children cheerfully cheered heartily as the coaches passed through the main streets of Lydd.

The first stop was made at Rolvenden, and an hour later another at Blackboys, where refreshments were given on the village green. The children left a good impression on the villagers, for it was noticeable that when the coaches moved off not a scrap of rubbish could be seen. All the children were warmly welcomed at Haywards Heath, and were largely conveyed in private cars to the houses of their foster parents. Nurses were in attendance and Boy Scouts carried the luggage of the smaller children.

To the children it seemed a great adventure. That first night enemy planes attacked Haywards Heath, but fortunately the parents knew nothing about it. The majority of the children soon settled down but for a few it was too much and they returned to their parents and the Marsh.

Officially, the Battle of Britain is considered to have taken place between 8 August and 31 October. Romney Marsh and south-east England bore the main impact. At times an alert would last all day; on other occasions the sirens sounded so often that the alerts became mixed up with the all-clears. And so many incidents occurred that many went unreported.

Lydd schoolchildren, all labelled and carrying their luggage and gas masks, wait patiently for coaches to evacuate them to Haywards Heath, Sussex, 10 August 1940.

Lydd and New Romney schoolchildren who have stopped for lunch at Blackboys, East Sussex, on their journey to Haywards Heath.

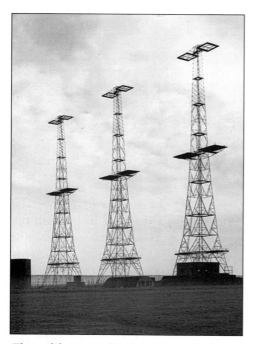

Three of the seven tall radar towers at East Guldeford that gave warning of approaching enemy aircraft. Built in 1939, the station was dismantled in about 1960.

On 12 August just before 7 a.m., raiders came in between St Mary's Bay and New Romney. Although challenged by a squadron of Spitfires and driven off, they managed to drop a number of bombs in the area of Caldecott Lane, Westbroke, Lydd before departing towards Rye. Another flight of enemy planes bombed the coast, fracturing a gas main at Littlestone and hitting Maddieson's Holiday Camp at Greatstone. Houses at Dungeness, Littlestone and Brookland all suffered damage. In the afternoon all coastal areas were targeted again. This day is particularly remembered for attacks on the radar stations, and those at Dover, Rye and Pevensey were hit. The Rye station plotted three aircraft heading its way, and just after 9 a.m. three Messerschmitt Me110s began a dive-bombing attack, killing two WAAFs and causing considerable damage. The raiders, led by Oblt Wilhelm Roissiger, met a barrage of fire from the anti-aircraft defence, and as soon as they had dropped their bombs they made for the coast. The station resumed normal service within a few hours.

One British bomber, a Whitley, hit while returning from a target in Occupied Europe in the early hours of 14 August, crashed into the sea between Dymchurch and Hythe. Dungeness lifeboat *Charles Cooper Henderson* put to sea with Coxswain Doug Oiller in command at 5.50 a.m. and found that a small Hythe fishing boat belonging to Buller Griggs had gone to the rescue. Two of the airmen owed their lives to Buller Griggs, ex-coxswain of Hythe lifeboat, who had been dismissed from the lifeboat service – many believed unjustly – earlier in the year. He had said at the time that he would 'go to sea in my own boat to save lives'. His crew were his son A. Griggs, nephew W. Griggs, cousin R. Griggs, M. Cloke and B. Cloke. Dungeness lifeboat towed them ashore. The third airman was rescued by Miss Peggy Prince of The Cabin, Dymchurch. She put to sea at first in a small canoe with a soldier as crewman, but they could not find the airman and returned to shore. Then he was sighted by someone with a telescope and, although it was very choppy, she promptly put to sea again, this time on her own. She located the airman, somehow got him aboard her frail craft, and made it safely to land. The airman was taken to her house until an ambulance arrived. Miss Prince was awarded the BEM for her bravery.

Miss Peggy Prince who bravely put to sea in her canoe to rescue Sgt J. Marshall, the wireless operator of a Whitley bomber that was forced to ditch off Dymchurch.

The morning of Thursday 15 August was fairly quiet, but just after 3 p.m. the sirens began wailing as raiders approached. Twelve bombs and fifteen parachute bombs were dropped in the Dymchurch area. At 6.30 p.m. six Dornier Do17s flew west low over Lydd Camp, pursued by Hurricanes, and later bombs were dropped in a line opposite Caldecott Farm, Lydd, falling into a drainage dyke but without exploding. More bombs were seen to fall in the New Romney area but no damage was sustained.

Sunday 18 August was a costly day for the RAF, with the loss of 15 airmen, but much more so for the Luftwaffe, who had 125 killed in air battles over Britain on that day, according to Air Ministry accounts. The sirens sounded all day throughout Kent and Sussex, and the whole of the south-east suffered loss of life and severe damage. Clifford Bloomfield, in his book *Wings over Rye*, writes about that day:

It was on Sunday lunchtime that bombs were dropped on Rye for the first time. The German bombers were returning back from a raid and, as I watched them from the entrance of the garden shelter, they flew low over the town. I did not see the bombs drop but the line of the stick can easily be traced today. If one starts at Godfreys (now the council lock-up garages), then to the Mint, where two bombs exploded front and back on the open site adjacent to No. 47, which had been a dwelling and also the Police Inspector's office at one time. Francis Sinden and his family were bombed out there. The next to be hit was across the road to the rear and side of Faraday House, then No. 2 Mermaid Street and finally the garden room of Lamb House, which was demolished. Other bombs dropped in the area of Udimore Road and the Old Brickyards. People killed this day were Mr G. Bumstead, Mrs F. Bumstead, Mr J.H. Bumstead and Mr N.C. Firrell.

The serious damage done to the Mermaid Inn after an air raid on Rye on 18 August 1940.

In Kent a crippled Messerschmitt Me110 crash-landed at Dering Farm, Lydd, and pilot Ruediger Proske and his radio operator, who was badly injured, were taken prisoner. At about the same time a Heinkel 111, piloted by Rudolf Ahens, crash-landed at Snargate. The crew tried to set fire to their plane but were captured by the Army. One of them died later in Rye Memorial Hospital. All five aboard a Dornier Do17 that plunged into the sea off Dungeness were killed, as were the two crew members of a Messerschmitt Me110 which crashed on the edge of the Marsh at Bonnington. The crew of another Messerschmitt were more fortunate – both escaped unhurt when their aircraft was shot down at Newchurch. Two other airmen in a further Messerschmitt who escaped without serious injury were returning from a raid when their plane was hit by anti-aircraft fire as it passed over Brookland. Flying low in trouble over Lydd Camp, it was again fired on by Canadian troops carrying out Bren-gun training on the ranges, and crash-landed minutes later at Dengemarsh. Four lads, Bob Galloway, Billy and Charlie Wren and Jack Carpenter, were out rabbiting in the vicinity. Jack recalls:

First we heard gunfire from the camp; it was very close to the control tower. We saw tracers hit the German plane and it came down at Podhill. We went across and we saw someone helping the crewmen out. One had been shot in the leg. The crew of a searchlight battery at Brickwall Farm came tearing across and told us they would take

Bomb damage to the High Street, Dymchurch, 24 August 1940. Many buildings were destroyed, including the Arcade.

over. We hadn't even spoken to the Germans. Suddenly we heard this roar; there were hundreds of Canadian troops running towards us. They had been using the ranges and were in one big mass. These Canadians almost stripped the plane, taking everything as souvenirs. The camera and the gun went. Suddenly some British officers arrived. They told the Canadians to leave things alone; they were told to sod off. These Canadians believed they had shot down the German plane with their Bren guns.

On 20 August police notified the public that for the next two days guns of the 43rd Wessex Division would be practice-firing from inland over Littlestone and Greatstone and out to sea. Also, from Old Romney and Midley, they would be shelling the area which is now the RSPB reserve – making it necessary for the Prebble family at Dengemarsh to go to Lydd during daylight as a precaution.

Six incendiary bombs apparently aimed at the Rye radar station on 22 August fell harmlessly short in farmland. Meanwhile, a British convoy making its way down the Channel had to run the gauntlet of shells fired from the French coast. Air battles raged overhead and a casualty was 754728 Plt Off J.R. Morrison, who baled out near Newchurch but was killed when his parachute failed to open. On 24 August – a day when the sirens sounded continuously and the Marsh folk spent many hours in their shelters – Dymchurch suffered badly. Mr Alfred Austin, aged fifty-six, and his wife Ada, aged fifty-three, were both killed when a bomb hit their home Sea Breeze – the first local civilian fatalities caused by enemy action. Heavy damage was inflicted by bombs that fell on the outfall bridge at the village entry from New Romney, in the street near the bus station, at Sellinge Farm on the St Mary-in-the-Marsh road and close to the fire station. Another device landed near the parish church but failed to explode and was later defused.

Mr and Mrs Austin lost their lives when a bomb flattened this house, Sea Breeze, in Dymchurch on 24 August 1940.

Despite the air raids of 24 August, farmers and buyers turned out as usual for the annual New Romney Sheep Fair, held on the fairground in Fairfield Road, and Messrs Finn-Kelcey and A. Finn sold a thousand ewes and lambs. Although movement restrictions kept Midlands buyers away, good prices were paid, with ewes reaching 60s a head and lambs 45s; this was an increase of nearly 3s a head compared to the previous year. It was on this day, too, that the announcement was made of the award of the Victoria Cross to Flt Lt Roderick Alister Brook Learoyd, whose parents lived at Frogs Hall, New Romney. The citation said Learoyd had shown 'conspicuous bravery' in a daring raid on the Dortmund to Ems canal. Flt Lt Learoyd had been flying a Hampden I and their task had been to bomb the twin-aqueducts that carry the canal across the Ems river. There was fierce ground fire and some of the bombers were shot down. Learoyd's aircraft was hit several times and he was blinded by searchlights, but he held course and flew on determinedly through the flak until his bombs were released.

Enemy planes that had probably failed to reach their target jettisoned fourteen bombs over Brookland as they headed back to France at 2.40 a.m. on 27 August. All landed on farmland, but Lydd firemen were called out a little later to deal with incendiaries that had started fires between Caldicott Crossing and Lydd station. The last day of August was one of a series of air battles as the RAF challenged hundreds of enemy aircraft passing over the Marsh on their way to targets further inland. A Messerschmitt Me109 crashed into holly trees near the Wicks on Lydd Ranges. The pilot was taken prisoner, as were the four crew members of a Dornier bomber brought down at Newchurch. The pilot escaped when a Spitfire crashed at Hope Farm, Snargate, and Flt Lt F.M. Smith, a Canadian, baled out wounded and badly burned, but lived to fly again, when his Spitfire came down at New Romney after combat over Dungeness.

In the first few days of September five British aircraft and four German planes came down in various parts of the Marsh. A Dornier DO17 crashed at 2.36 p.m. in Tarts Field beside the Dungeness–Lydd road near the beach quarry and was totally wrecked. The crew – one of them injured – were taken to Lydd Camp. A Hurricane fell in flames near Swamp Crossing, Midley, but the pilot, Flg Off Carswell, managed to bale out and landed at New Romney suffering from burns and a wounded leg. On 5 September local farmer Mr H.J. Blacklocks reported to the ARP centre that he had five planes down on his land: a Messerschmitt at

Dengemarsh; a Dornier Do17 at Tarts Field; a Spitfire at Nine Acres, New Romney; a Spitfire at Burmarsh; and another Spitfire at Newchurch. An Army officer performed a humane duty on 5 September when he shot the pilot of a Messerschmitt Me109 which had crashed in flames in Kingsmarsh Lane, Midley. Brave attempts had been made to rescue him but the fire was too intense.

The threat of a German invasion was still there, although Hitler's boast that the war would be over by 15 August had proved hollow. It is now known that the flat stretch of coast between Folkestone and Hastings was to have been the landing place for his troops. Since the beginning of September the intelligence services had reported tugs, barges, landing craft, launches and gunboats converging on the ports of Holland, Belgium and northern France. Bomber Command began to counter these movements by attacks on the ports. Ben Tart, up in his Observer Corps post at Dungeness, commented: 'Out

Bomb damage at The Arcade, Dymchurch, 24 August 1940.

The Dornier shot down on 1 September 1940 in Tarts Field, Dungeness Road, Lydd, by Sammy Allard of 85 Squadron. The German pilot, Mathias Maossen, was wounded. Of his crew, Wilhelm Illy was unhurt, Heinrich Wöhner wounded and Gels Speiss killed.

went all these bombers; they played hell with Calais and Boulogne harbours. We stood up in the Observer Post; it was a clear night and we could see the planes caught in the searchlights and the ack-ack going up. You could also see the fires; it was a wonder anything was left.'

Had the invasion taken place, would the Germans have been victorious? Opinion is divided. The Navy still ruled the Channel and the RAF were doing well in the sky. On land the 43rd Wessex Division, responsible at the time for the defence of the stretch of coastline between Hastings and Folkestone, had been preparing for several months. The Royal Artillery had been practising firing guns out to sea, with their batteries reinforced by a detachment of the Newfoundland Artillery, dug in near New Romney. Mr F. Dicks, then a soldier in the Royal Fusiliers, writes of his memories of that time: 'I was in the Intelligence section, whose job was the defence of Dungeness beach against enemy invasion. The tower of All Saints, Lydd, is the highest point on Romney Marsh and we were using the top of the tower as an observation post, noting the enemy activity in the Channel, and especially looking for a signal from our own craft to warn that an invasion had started. I also remember lying on the beach at Dungeness with a rifle and five rounds of ammunition to repel the enemy. When we were relieved we had to hand over the ammunition to the next lot.'

Mr A.T. Franklin, a soldier in the 18th Battalion, Royal Fusiliers, was put to work on the coastal defences: 'Active service for the battalion started each morning just before daybreak, when we stood to, looking seawards for the Germans. Our main task was the fortification of the coast from Dungeness to Dymchurch. A party of six or so would be left at Dungeness digging large holes in the shingle along the beach. A Royal Engineers corporal said the holes were to take large concrete pipes set at an angle, with a charge at the bottom, and then filled with shingle, to be fired at the Germans should they try to land.' Ex-army personnel in correspondence with the author say they all thought the Navy would prevent an invasion – and all hoped that the High Command had more adequate forces located on the surrounding hills.

The air battles continued. Twelve bombs fell close to Midley Poorhouses on 6 September; a thousand-pounder failed to explode, and although bomb disposal teams tried to defuse it, it kept sinking into the clay soil until it was beyond reach. A further rash of minefields on the south-east side of Lydd brought a warning from the military stating: 'All personnel should be warned against crossing minefields under any circumstances before permission has been received from the military.' Seemingly it was all right to be blown up provided you had obtained permission.

On 11 September a Hurricane of 504 Squadron was shot down during an air battle and plunged into the ground and burned out at Newchurch. Plt Off Arthur William Clarke was killed. On 11 September 1986 a headstone was erected close to the site of the crash, as it was the wish of his family that his remains should be left there undisturbed. On that same day in 1940 an air battle between Hurricanes and Junkers Ju88s claimed the life of 24-year-old Polish Sgt Plt Stanislaw Duszynsii, whose damaged plane plunged into the ground at Little Scotney, Midley. His body lies at rest at the site.

Humour, happily, managed to survive September's grim days. Mrs Chubb remembers: 'I was sitting chatting to two of the older fishermen characters outside one of the Dungeness cottages

The memorial stone to Arthur William Clarke, which is at the roadside on the approach to Newchurch from St Mary-in-the-Marsh. Plt Off Clarke was killed when the Hurricane he was in crashed at Newchurch.

on a form – they all had forms outside – and this air battle was going on. One of these old fellows remarked to the other, "One of these days somebody's going to get bloody well hurt."'

On 18 September the Police warned that objects had been dropped by parachute over the Marsh and it was believed that these were magnetic mines. It was advised that all metal objects should be kept away from them. A description issued later that day said they were dark-green cylinders, 8 × 2 ft, with a fuse marked Y22.34 with FB1940 below. Two that exploded formed a crater 1,000 ft in diameter.

On 21 September the popular vicar of Warehorne, the Revd Dr Walter George Ivens, aged seventy, was cycling to Brenzett Church, against a strong wind, to take a service there. As he neared Brenzett enemy aircraft appeared overhead, so he pedalled all the harder. During the singing of the hymn 'Lead us, heavenly Father, lead us', Dr Ivens

German pilot F.W. Briedrich unhurt but under guard after his Heinkel was brought down at Burmarsh, 11 September 1940.

swayed and fell; his exhausting ride from Warehorne had put too much strain on his heart.

Despite the air raids and a shortage of labour, the Marsh farmers had to harvest their much-needed crops. Many of the fields had unexploded bombs in them, and farmer Claude

Paine asked the military to clear one at Brookland so that his potatoes could be dug. On this occasion prompt action was taken; in other cases farmers had to wait, so some of them took a chance, or the workers did. Farmworker Jack Flisher remembers going very gingerly up and down the rows in a field where a string of bombs had fallen, his bottom not quite touching the tractor seat. Farmworker Duggie Apps had an encounter with live bombs: 'I remember one time we were picking up potatoes at Soccar Leas, Belgar, a party of us, women as well. Over came Jerry and he dropped a couple of bombs in the field; ah, big ones at that, pretty near big enough to get a horse in the crater. We all hit the ground between the tater rows, as if that was going to save us. The horses bolted; it frightened us, let alone them. The only bruises we had were from flying potatoes.'

On 27 September a number of Junkers Ju88s made a sweep towards New Romney, where two bombs were dropped. Ack-ack guns opened fire from various points and the planes turned back across the Channel. Later, another Ju88, returning crippled from a raid inland, fell into the sea just south of Galloways. The crew, Fw Sergocke and Uffz Schmidt, were rescued. On the same day three workmen were injured, one seriously, by a landmine explosion at Littlestone. An inquest was held on 28 September at Lydd town hall on Pte William Gordon McGowan, aged twenty-one, killed while filling sandbags. He was at the bottom of a pit 7 ft deep when the sides caved in and buried him.

On 30 September three more soldiers were killed. George Ernest Hillby, aged twenty-two, and Joseph William Slater, aged twenty-three, both of the Royal Artillery, died when a shell they were examining exploded on Lydd Ranges. A soldier of the Somerset Light Infantry died through stepping on a landmine at Dungeness. In the afternoon two RAF pilots had narrow escapes when they were shot down. Plt Off J. Radomsky, in a Hurricane, crash-landed on the shingle at Boulderwall Farm, Lydd, after tangling with a Messerschmitt Me109, and Plt Off V. Ortmans, also in a Hurricane, crash-landed at Galloways, falling to the fire power of a Dornier Do17. Both escaped unhurt.

A woman who did not follow the established procedure for visiting the area was equally lucky not to be fatally injured. She had had permission to visit her holiday home for a few hours to check that everything was all right, but she failed to report to the police station. Early in the afternoon police were called to the cottage at Dungeness. When Sgt Tye and PC F. Jones arrived a group of soldiers were standing a short distance away. Fred Jones recounts:

As a result of the many plane crashes and injuries to service personnel it was decided to have a mobile medical unit, fully equipped and staffed by a trained nurse. But because this large vehicle was unable to get to remote Marsh areas it was withdrawn after a few months. Those who operated unit No. 15 were, left to right: Miss Cape-Procter, Mrs Hughes, Mrs Fowle, Miss Tart and Miss Sweetman.

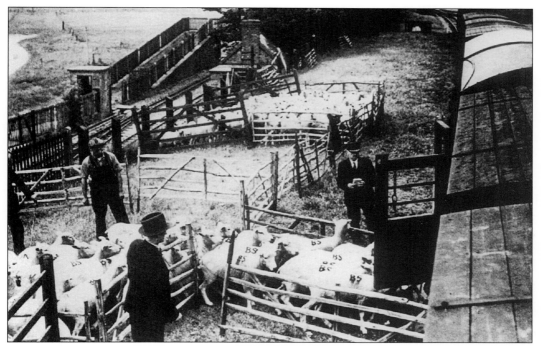

The evacuation of Romney Marsh sheep to the safety of the West Country, New Romney station, September 1940. Each sheep was marked with a broad arrow on the rear of its back.

On our arrival a Royal Engineers officer came forward to meet us and told us a woman was in a cottage in which a booby trap had been set. Sgt Tye asked him if anything had been done.

'Nothing,' he replied, 'we are frightened to do anything. I set a trap inside. She is moving around; she is bound to go up.'

So Sgt. Tye went up to the door and pushed it open. The woman was seated at her table having a bite to eat.

'Hello, my gal,' he said.

She replied 'Hello, Sergeant.'

'Why didn't you come and see me before you came on down here?'

She replied: 'Well, they didn't give me enough time to be here.'

Sgt. Tye: 'You were given a special time and you were told to report to me. You've done wrong, gal, and I tell you what I want you to do – you get up and walk straight towards me.'

'That's easy,' she said.

'I hope so,' he replied.

She got up and came straight out of the door. Sgt Tye told the officer to make safe the device. He then told the woman and she fainted on the spot. She had been walking all around it; did everything but step on it.

SIX

OCTOBER TO DECEMBER 1940

Although the final months of 1940 saw fewer air attacks on Romney Marsh the civilian casualties were the area's worst of the war. Lydd suffered its heaviest civilian fatalities in the early evening of Saturday 5 October. Five Messerschmitt 109s, plotted by the Brookland Observer Corps coming from the Rye area, turned at Midley and released their bombs over the south-west end of the town. Some fell near the Sergeants' Mess at the corner of Lydd Camp, injuring several soldiers; one scored a direct hit on two houses in Skinner Road; and another struck the home of Mr Thomas Stanley in the Back Lane (now Robin Hood Lane).

The Skinner Road bomb killed Mrs Isobel Ruth Bates and Mrs Kate Florence Perry, and Mr George Perry died later in hospital. Mr Graham Bates was seriously hurt but recovered. Mr Walter Nash, aged thirty-two, who was standing outside Mr Stanley's house, died from his injuries. The most fortunate was Nancy Pope, a young girl working for Mr and Mrs Bates, who was preparing a salad at the kitchen window when the bomb fell. Its blast knocked her down but she was shielded from the falling masonry by a piano. Mrs Nancy McGhie, as she is now, does not remember the blast but remembers being pulled out of the wreckage by a young boy named Reg Browning and Mr George Newton.

Remains of houses in Skinner Road, Lydd, where the town suffered its heaviest civilian casualties, 5 October 1940. The Army camp on the left of the photograph was badly hit in the same enemy raid.

The late Mrs Alice Coleman, who then lived close by in the back lane, now Robin Hood Lane, wrote down her memories of the raid:

It was a lovely day. But I had just returned from shopping when all hell let loose. We heard the first bomb drop; all our plates and china crashed to the floor. We lay between the sofa and the table. We pushed the children under the sofa. Out of the corner of my eye I saw our sideboard blown to bits. I don't know how many bombs there were or how long it lasted, but suddenly it all went quiet and we all got up, glad to be alive and unhurt. The children had small cuts on their knees where we had pushed them under the sofa.

I moaned over the sofa many times, but I feel it saved our lives; when we looked there were bullet holes along the arms. We got out into the garden and the house was wrecked. Just then Isobel Stanley came running to us; could we come to this man who was injured. We went with her and, outside her house, on the side of the road, was Walter Nash, very badly injured. It appears he was going to Tom Stanley for his wages. I shall never forget him or his mother, she was so upset. An officer and a party of soldiers came to help us try to retrieve our belongings.

On the same day the Dungeness lifeboat was called out when a plane was seen to crash into the sea during an air battle. Coxswain Oiller's log reads: 'At 2.10 p.m. I received a telephone message from Coastguard Lade stating a fighter aircraft had crashed in the sea about three miles off Lade. I at once went to our station and assembled crew and helpers and launched. We proceeded to the position given and found a German pilot, Uffz H. Bley, in a small rubber boat. We got him into the lifeboat, where we disarmed him and bandaged his head, which was cut. On returning we handed him over to a military guard.'

As the immediate threat of an invasion waned, some of the troops were moved inland. Mr F. Dicks recalls: 'We moved back to form a defensive line behind the Military Canal. The bridges over the canal were mined. My section were in an orchard at Bonnington, and in the course of our training we visited most of the Marsh villages. I remember a bus service which ran along the coast road between Folkestone and Lydd. These East Kent Company buses were bright red!' This latter piece of information is unusual. These double-deckers were visible from afar, yet most transport was camouflaged at this time.

German pilot Uffz H. Bley being brought ashore in the Dungeness lifeboat after being rescued from the Channel, 5 October 1940.

Meanwhile, steps to strengthen the coastal defences continued, with the larger buildings near the shore reinforced with concrete to house larger guns. The Arcade at Dymchurch, bus shelters and even haystacks became strong points. Because of the continual bombing of Lydd Camp a large number of troops were moved out and billeted in the town, taking over all the houses left empty by people who had evacuated the area. Meals for them were cooked in the empty school or at the Old Brewery, and also at the New Inn in South Street.

The devastation at Lydd church when a Me109 fighter-bomber scored a direct hit on the chancel, completely destroying it, 15 October 1940.

The headquarters and first-aid post for the St John Ambulance Brigade were in Lydd British Legion Hall. This is where both civilian and military casualties were first taken to be treated by local doctors Rupert and Edgar Palmer. The ambulances – converted cars – were driven by volunteers Ted Vidler, Ernest Paine, Miss Doris Mittell and Miss Helen Bailey. Mrs Pam Winkfield (née Adams), a St John member, recalls:

I remember an incident when they asked for volunteers as there was a young lady with her elderly mother still living on the coast. The mother was incapacitated and a mine had broken loose and was bobbing about on the foreshore right in front of their cottage and in danger of going up. It was high tide, and with a terrific gale blowing, so they asked for volunteers. Ted Vidler – he was good like that – volunteered immediately, and I thought I might as well go with him.

We had to have passes to go through the manned gate at the Halfway Bush on the Dungeness road. The guards saw us coming and waved 'goodbye' as they had heard what we had come for. Anyway, we managed to get this woman out and into the ambulance. We got back to the gate and stopped to chat to the guards – and the blooming mine went up. We looked back and all the roof of the cottage was going up. We had a lucky escape.

Mr and Mrs W. Tyrell's house in Station Road, Lydd, which received a direct hit from an enemy bomb on 13 October 1940. Miraculously, nobody was seriously injured.

Lydd church was damaged on 15 October. A direct bomb-hit completely destroyed the chancel and badly affected many other parts of the building. Another bomb struck the Station Road home of Mr and Mrs Tyrell and a third fell on Lydd Camp. Miraculously, nobody was seriously injured. Mr F. Dicks, who was one of the soldiers on duty on the church tower, wrote of his experience:

This particular day, among other enemy aircraft, three German fighter-bombers flew over us in the direction of London. A few minutes later they returned. One plane dropped his bombs on the outskirts of Lydd, the next two bombs were closer, and the third plane hit the church with its bomb. We could see the bombs falling, but luckily for us they hit the church away from the tower. One of our mates was practising playing the organ; he dived under the pews, buried but safe. The tower was blocked with debris and we had to be dug out. I was bomb-happy for many days. We actually felt the tower sway with the blast. I didn't go up the tower again.

On the 20 October Lydd Camp was again targeted; eighteen bombs were dropped and there were many casualties. Pam Winkfield, on duty at the British Legion Hall, recalls this incident: 'Many of the casualties were brought to the hall and there were so many we had to help attend them. Doctors Rupert and Edgar Palmer had to cope with them all. There were Canadians in the camp at this time and quite a few were killed. At the hall we had to

Noble's Garage at the west end of Lydd was hit by a high explosive (HE) bomb on 28 October 1940. Mr and Mrs Bob Noble were unhurt, having taken shelter in their cellar.

pick the shrapnel out of their wounds, and one little Canadian said to me, 'I want that shrapnel, miss,' so I had to wrap it up and give it to him to take home as a souvenir.'

The drill during an air raid was to take shelter, but on 22 October it cost three New Romney workmen their lives. The dug-out in which they were sheltering received a direct hit, killing Bertie George Ralph, aged fifty-seven, and Cecil Edward Sims, aged forty-one, both of Sussex Road, and Leonard Richard Summers, of The Avenue, Littlestone. Lydd suffered a further attack on 28 October. Of the twelve bombs dropped, one destroyed the home and garage business of Mr Bob Noble, another fell in the grounds of The Paddock, a third wrecked a house in Station Road and the remainder fell on the outskirts. Also, the High Street was machine-gunned.

A local war hero received a rather hot reception when he flew in on 2 November to receive the Freedom of the Borough of New Romney. Flt Lt Learoyd, who had won the Victoria Cross in September, was planning to land at Hawkinge, and on the way, at 3.20 p.m., he twice circled above his home in New Romney in a Hampden Mk1 night bomber. But he had to beat a hasty retreat when he came under fire from the anti-aircraft defences.

The body of a German soldier, aged about thirty, and dressed in a grey uniform, was washed ashore at Littlestone on 5 November. It had been in the sea for about eight weeks. There were no signs of injury and death was due to drowning. It was thought probable the man was one of the invasion force on which the RAF inflicted heavy casualties when they bombed the French ports. His body was buried at New Romney. Two days later the body of a German airman in flying kit was washed ashore on Lade sands. His jacket bore a medal ribbon for the Polish Campaign. The same day a number of bombers approaching the coast were identified as twin-engine Italian Savoias, but as soon as they encountered heavy ack-ack fire they turned back across the Channel.

Mrs Nell Prebble milking her goat Sandy McNab. Sadly, Sandy was blown up by a mine on 19 October 1941.

The 5th Battalion, The Somerset Light Infantry, were relieved by The Queen's Regiment on 12 November, having been on the Marsh since June. As they waited on Lydd station for trains an aerial battle began overhead, with the Germans unaware of the tempting target below. Later in the month the body of a British soldier, Gunner William Arthur Hayhoe, was washed ashore near the Martello tower, Sands Estate, Dymchurch, on 20 November; the cause of death was drowning.

December was fairly quiet on the whole, with just a few areas targeted. The 10th was notable for being the day when two of the four spies caught on Romney Marsh, José Waldberg, aged twenty-five, and Carl Meir, aged twenty-four, were hanged at Pentonville Prison. On 17 December Charles Kieboom, aged twenty-eight, was also hanged. On that day a Wellington bomber of 99 Squadron crashed in the early hours in Kings Avenue, Rye, after running out of fuel. The pilot was Sgt C.F. Muller. On 30 December F.W. Schmidtt was taken prisoner when his plane crashed at Wheelsgate Farm, Old Romney. It had been a very harrowing and anxious year. Mrs Nell Prebble summed it up as she ended her diary:

Goodbye and good riddance to a ROTTEN YEAR.

SEVEN

BRITISH RESISTANCE

Only now, more than fifty years after Dunkirk, are the full details emerging of one of the Second World War's best-kept secrets – the formation of a clandestine army, the British Resistance, pledged to harry the Germans if they set foot in this country. By May 1940 Hitler's army had overrun Holland and Belgium and by the end of June France had fallen. The Germans now lined the coast on the other side of the Channel. An invasion seemed imminent, and the task of organizing the defence of an ill-armed Britain fell to General Sir Edmund Ironside.

The 1st London Division, responsible for holding the area from Sheppey in Kent to Rye in East Sussex, only had eleven 25-pounder field guns, no anti-tank guns and a mere twenty-one Bren-gun carriers. And in order to move troops, civilian vehicles – mainly coaches – had to be hired. The Home Guard, already in existence, was equally short of weapons, so it was originally decided not to try to defend Romney Marsh but to make a stand on the line of the Royal Military Canal.

By September, with the Germans still hesitating, and with more war materials available, this decision was reversed. An invasion still seemed certain, so Winston Churchill gave orders for the formation of a British Resistance. As many as 3,500 men were recruited, all of them country men, all hand-picked for their local knowledge and their ability, if necessary, to live off the land. And they were trained by commandos to be saboteurs. It was all very hush-hush; for safety's sake not even the men's families were told. And although they came under its umbrella, they had no connection with the local Home Guard, which was kept in ignorance of their existence.

The badge of recognition for members of the Auxiliary Units, although many did not receive it until the war was over. The badge of recognition was a small lapel badge that identified which unit you belonged to.

The job of setting up the British Resistance was given to Maj Colin McVean Gubbins of Military Intelligence, with headquarters at Coleshill House, near Swindon, Wiltshire. All units throughout Britain were eventually grouped into three battalions: 201 (Scotland), 202 (Essex to South Wales) and 203 (south of the Thames). A regional training centre for Sussex and Kent was organized by a Grenadier Guards captain, Peter Fleming (brother of James Bond author Ian Fleming) at The Garth, a farmhouse at Bilting, near Wye. His orders were to train small teams whose role it would be to operate behind the German lines at night sabotaging tanks, lorries, ammunition dumps and small enemy posts.

40

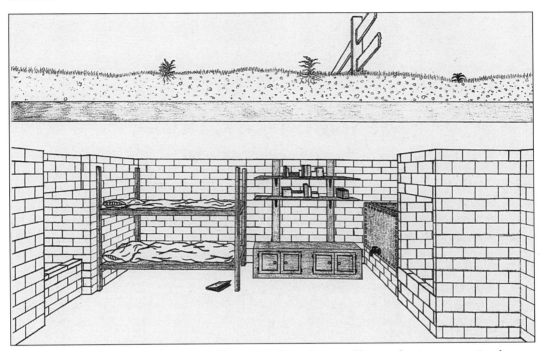

A drawing of the Snargate Auxiliary Unit bunker, which shows the general layout when it was operational. Drawn by Jeremy Cole.

The Kent and Sussex Auxiliary Units, as they later became known, were some of the first to be set up and Peter Fleming's ideas became the pattern for the rest of the British Isles. Taking over in 1941, Captain Norman Field established three patrols on Romney Marsh: the Mushroom Patrol at Snargate, the Truffle Patrol near New Romney and the Toadstool Patrol inland from Dymchurch. At the time of writing this book information has come to light of a patrol in Lydd, but it would appear that the members have taken their secrets to the grave.

The three Operational Bases, designed by Captain Field and built by Corbens of Maidstone, were identical in size, being 20 ft long, 8 ft wide and 8 ft high. The external walls were of reinforced concrete lined with bitumen, and white bricks were used on the inside, with a ventilating downpipe in each corner and three air outlets along the centre of the chamber. There was an entrance at either end, with dwarf walls at the bottom in case the enemy should drop a grenade into the entrance shaft. Iron bars were let into the shaft brickwork to form steps. The entrances had camouflaged wooden covers.

The Mushroom Patrol at Snargate, with its OB close to the village, was led by Dick Body, a Marsh farmer, who recalls how he came to be involved.

In 1941 I was approached by Capt Allnat, who, like me, had been released from 468 Searchlight Company Territorials to resume civil occupation. He asked me if I was in the Home Guard. On being told yes, he replied 'That does not matter.' He wanted to know if I could find six more men and undertake a job in this area, the emphasis being on good local knowledge. He could not tell me more, but if I could not find enough men he could put me on to two. I was soon able to say yes and would be glad of the two men.

Shortly after this I was asked to take my party up to The Garth at Bilting. There, after reading a copy of the Official Secrets Act and, I think, signing that we had read it, we were told what we had let ourselves in for. The following men were recruited: Percy Town, Fred Cottingham, George Elvy, Alfred Jemison, Henry Ovenden, Bill Brotherwood and later, Vic Cripps.

The Truffle Patrol at New Romney, with its OB at Old Romney, was led by Percy Clark of New Romney.

I was working at the time for George Palmer in his corn store in New Romney. I was out and when I got back a message had been left at the office for me to ring a field number, and I rang this number and they wondered if they could come down and interview me at 2 o'clock that afternoon.

Four people came down and the first thing they told me was they were going to start this organization which was secret and before they told me anything about it I had to

The surviving members of the Marsh auxiliary units in 1994. Left to right: Dick Body (Snargate), Percy Clark (New Romney), George Elvy (Snargate) and Gordon Prior (New Romney). Sadly, Dick died in 1997 at the age of ninety-two.

sign on the dotted line. They then told me what they wanted and asked me if I could get a patrol going within forty-eight hours so that I could report to headquarters at The Garth on the Sunday morning. I was asked to select people we could trust and we could work with. I made my selection and nobody refused when I asked them.

We went to Wye on the Sunday morning and assembled in this hall and we were told part of it. Then we had to sign the Secrets Act again and then we were told exactly what they wanted us to do. We had no choice once we had signed. The men I selected were: Charlie Veness, Thomas Wimble, Frank Carey, Ray Fagg, Jack Lancaster, Ted Bolton and later Gordon Prior and Francis Carey.

George Elvy, who was a looker (a certain type of shepherd common in the Romney Marsh area) living at Brookland, remembers:

I was already in the Home Guard at Snargate, which at that time was run by Dick Body. He called me to one side on the quiet and said 'Would you come down to my place on such-and-such a night?' When I got there, there were some of the other lads in the Home Guard and Dick gave us a lecture on what he wanted. When we all agreed he said we would not be going to the Home Guard meetings any more; our meetings would be at his house. Dick made arrangements for us to go to The Garth for training. We all signed the Secrets Act.

Many wondered why we left the Home Guard but we could not tell them, it was so secret. The Bunker or OB, as we referred to it, was built after we were formed. We went over there several times and all slept there one night and did a scheme from it. After one night on the boards of the bunks we set to work and replaced them with sheep wire-netting. Everything was in place and ready.

On Sunday mornings we would go to The Garth for special training with live explosives. We were taught to lay charges so that, for instance, a tree could be made to fall across the road, and the length of fuse necessary for us to reach safety. We occasionally trained with the Regular Army, but with dummy explosives, and were sent to put explosives on lorries, guns and tanks, where they were going to do most damage. The Army would then inspect to see that we had done the job right.

We also used to camouflage up and creep up to a nearby Army unit. They would be told in advance and we would see how close we could get. On one particular day I was creeping up to a searchlight battery near The Bull at Newchurch. I was by the road in a dik [dyke]. I heard footsteps and lay perfectly still, but I was spotted by a lady passer-by who called out, 'You poor man'. She thought I had been in an accident and been thrown in the ditch. That put the kibosh on that exercise.

Everybody, including the Army, thought we were just Home Guards training. They knew nothing of our new role. We usually met for training once a week; we did our training in the area, mostly at night in the dark. Perhaps we wouldn't go to the OB for several months. Dick could check it regularly because it was on his land, so being there would not arouse suspicions. In the winter indoors at Dick's house we did map-reading. We also practised taking the weapons to pieces and putting them together again blindfolded, things like that. Dick was a good leader because he knew what he was doing.

We would practise with live ammunition, firing against a thick bank, and on one occasion the bank was so hard the bullets ricocheted over the top and a farmworker in the next field shouted 'Oi! These bullets are flying around everywhere!' We also made up a target like a man's head on a string, lay in the dik, and one man would pull on the string so that the head came up and you would use a revolver to fire at it. We would all take it in turns. That was our training with the revolver on a moving target. After a while we were quite good at it.

The surviving member of the Eastbridge Auxiliary Group, Albert Ovenden, at his home in Ramsgate, 1994.

Albert Ovenden, also a looker, lived at Eastbridge, inland from Dymchurch, and was a member of the Auxiliary Patrol Toadstool based at Eastbridge.

Don Symonds came to see me and asked me to join him and he explained as much as he knew or could. He told me it was secret and I was to tell no one. At the time I lived at Sankey Farm, I was looker foreman for Mr Hobbs. My brother Alfred was also recruited by Don Symonds, but we kept it quiet, not even my sister knew until you made the enquiry [November 1994].

I enjoyed the training at Bilting. That was usually on a Sunday. We were taught by the Lovat Scouts to blow up trees so that they fell on a certain part of a road as roadblocks, also to blow up a convoy of vehicles. They had some old vehicles in the woods to practise on, things like that. We very rarely went to our OB; we were told not to in case it was discovered and, as you know, it was by troops in 1944. We were then disbanded and returned to the Home Guard.

Dick Body remembers his role as patrol leader in great detail:

Soon the patrols were kitted out and training began at The Garth. Most of the practical work with explosives was done under Capt Field and a Royal Engineer corporal, and for weapon training, field craft, etc. under a Sgt MacDonald and Cpl MacKenzie of the Lovat Scouts. At times we handled captured German weapons so that we had a certain working knowledge of them. We were expected to practise in our own areas what we had learnt at The Garth.

Soon we were operational and were issued with quite a lot of material, which we took home so that we could practise and familiarize ourselves with it. The first time or two we handled gelignite very gingerly but soon learnt that all was safe so long as the basic rules were obeyed. We learnt the best places to immobilize tanks, vehicles, destroy stores, interrupt communications and set the various devices off by delay mechanisms, trip wires, etc., one of the important points being to do so in such a way that sabotage would not be too obvious.

Each member of the patrol had a .38 Smith & Wesson revolver and a knife as his personal weapons. Each patrol had as well a Thompson machine gun, two .300 Springfield rifles and a .22 Winchester magazine rifle with silencer and telescopic sight. This .22 was particularly for use against guard dogs and perhaps sentries. In 1944 our Thompson gun was withdrawn to send to Denmark and every man was issued with a Sten gun, a weapon they did not think much of; when you squeezed the trigger you did not know how many rounds you might fire.

For the first year no importance was put on dress and drill. Various members of patrols went on a weekend course at Coleshill. There everything was intensive, with the first lecture taking place during the Friday evening meal. The officers running the HQ had all their meals with us; at the first meal the colonel sat himself next to me. On the Saturday, lectures and practice went on all day with a night scheme that finished about 1 a.m., more lectures and demonstrations on the Sunday morning: unarmed combat with men from the Army Physical Training Corps, etc. After a quick meal we were trucked to the station and train back.

George Elvy and Dick Body at one of the two entrances to their auxiliary unit bunker at Snargate, 1994.

Every patrol which went to The Garth was marked for competence with explosives, weapon drill, cleanliness of weapons, firing and grenade throwing. After the first selecting round, patrols were graded A, B and C. Mushroom found themselves in C and something had to be done. So all weapons spent Saturday evening on the kitchen table being cleaned before going up to The Garth. As only five points were awarded for full turnout, and twenty for drill and turnout, there were occasional absentees. As a result of gamesmanship, Mushroom climbed by two steps from C to No. 4 in A.

Just before D-Day in 1944 a suggestion went around that volunteers might be dropped in France to aid the French Resistance. This was immediately squashed as we were only trained to know our own locality. Also at that time we were warned that possibly the Germans might make diversionary raids to hinder the D-Day preparations.

In November 1944, when all threat of invasion had ceased, the Auxiliary Units were stood down and all the operational stores were collected. The remaining practice material was disposed of. After the war a party of soldiers was sent round to deal with the OBs. The one at Old Romney, which was the New Romney base, was blown up and filled in. But when Dick Body was asked if he wanted his one at Snargate blown up and was told it would leave a large hole, he said 'Leave it alone.' The one at Eastbridge was closed in the early part of the war because of breach of security, so was not on the Army's destruction list. As a result two bases have survived to remind us of Britain's 'Secret Army'. Both now are classed as war monuments, but only the Eastbridge one can be visited.

New Romney Fire Brigade pumping out the bunker used by the Snargate Auxiliary Unit, 1994. Left to right: Dave Douglas, James Smart, Bernard Morris, Rod Groombridge and Tony Smart.

After pumping out the auxiliary unit's bunker at Snargate, Sub Officer Tony Smart (left) and Fireman Bernard Morris of New Romney Fire Brigade make sure it is safe to enter.

George Elvy (left), then aged seventy-eight, and Dick Body, ninety, the two surviving members of the auxiliary unit at Snargate, in the bunker after it had been pumped out, 8 September 1994.

This inventory of equipment was kept by Dick Body, leader of the Snargate Auxiliary Unit.

Auxiliary Units

Arms per Section (of 7 men)
1 Thompson Sub-Machine Gun
2 Rifles Springfield
2 Bayonets
7 Revolvers (1 per man)

7 Knives (fighting) & Sheath
48 Grenades
48 A.W. Bombs
3 Rubber Truncheons *+

Explosives
4 Small Aux. each contained (Sealed) in G.S. Tins
2 Fog Signals
12 2¾" lengths of match ended Bickford
1 Crimping Tool
6 Striker Boards
2 Boxes non-flaming fuses
1 Tube Vaseline
30 Copper Tube Ignitors
6 Spools Trip Wire .032"
6 Spools Trip Wire .014"
1 Coil Adhesive Tape

Ammunition
1200 rounds .45 per Thompson S.M.G.
50 rounds .300 per Rifle
50 Pull Switches
50 Pressure Switches
50 A.P. Mines *+

Anti-Gas
Cotton Waste

Clothing per Man
1 Suit Denim Overalls
1 B.D. Blouse
1 B.D. Trousers
1 Cap Forage
1 Pr. Boots
1 Pr. Laces
2 Pr. Titles, H.G.
1 Greatcoat D.M.
1 Pr. Rubber Boots
1 Steel Helmet

Equipment per Patrol
2 Scabbards
7 Holsters, Pistol
2 Slings Rifle
1 Gallon Rum *+
10 Gallons Paraffin
7 Water Sterilization Outfits
7 Composite Ration Packs
1 Pr. Wire Cutters
2 Gallon Tin Petrol
1 Periscope *+

Also 1 .22 Winchester Rifle & Silencer

Items with *+ not in fact issued

Thompson S.M.G. withdrawn in 1944 to be sent to Denmark, when Sten guns were issued.

Stores Received

2 prs Knuckledusters *+
15 S.T. Grenades *+
7 Sten Guns (issued later)

4 Large Magnets
36 Paraffin Incendiaries
18 1 lb Incendiaries
60 Time Pencils
48 Time Bickford Fuse
30 Time Instantaneous Fuse
25 Time Cordtex
22 detonators (2 magazines)
15 lbs Polar Gelignite
12 Sandbags

36 rounds .38 Revolver

50 Spare Detonators
50 Release Switches (issued later)

7 lbs Bleach

1 Pr. Anklets Leather
1 Belt Leather
1 Frog Leather
1 Dressing Field
2 Blankets, G.S.
1 Box Ointment A.G. No. 2
1 Sheets Ground
6 Eye Shields A.G.
1 Respirator A.A.

1 Sling Tommy Gun
1 First Aid Set (with Morphia)
1 Box Thompson S.M.G. & Spares
10 Magazines (20 rounds)
1 Monocular & Case
2 Don V Field Telephones
½ Mile Cable
2 Pullthroughs, Weights & Gauzes
7 Rods Pistol

Telescopic Sight & Magazine

Practice Stores Issued
Quantity

Quantity	Item		Quantity	Item
3 × 10	Wet gun cotton		1	Spade
2 × 10	Dry gun cotton		1	Pick & Helve
17	Large incendiaries		1	Auger
10	Paraffin incendiaries		1	Hurricane Lamp
5 × 10	Pressure switches		1	Tilley Lamp
4	Smoke canisters		1	Primus
50	Detonators		1	Kettle Camp
2 × 24	A.E. Bottles (phosphorus)		1	Elsan Closet
6 × 12	Mills grenades		1	Thermometer
6 × 10	Release switches		1	Compass
38 × 10	Lead delays, 3 hour		1	Monocular
37 × 10	Lead delays, 1 hour		12	Night Lights
1 × 21 lbs	Amatol (explosive)		10	Gallons Paraffin
1 × 7 lbs	Plastic (explosive)		2	Gallons Petrol
5 × 10	Pull switches		9	Tubes Camouflage Cream
1 × 10	Lead delays, 4 hour			
1 × 10	Lead delays, 1½ hour			
15	Aux Units Mark II (Operational)			
2	Aux Units Mark I (Operational)			

4 × 50 rounds .22 ammunition for .22 rifle
30 × 20 rounds 9 mm ammunition for Sten guns
20 × 50 rounds .45 ammunition for Thompson
10 × 20 rounds .45 ammunition for Machine Gun
2 × 40 rounds .38 ammunition for Revolver
4 × 20 rounds .300 ammunition for Springfield Rifle

EIGHT

1941

There was a relatively peaceful start to 1941; very cold north-easterly winds across Europe, accompanied by heavy snow, inhibited enemy air offensives. On Romney Marsh the weather was much the same, with deep drifts hampering travel. In fact on 8 February it was so cold at Lade and Dungeness that the sea froze, and so too did the shingle and sands as the tide receded. Fisherman Harry Young, digging for lugworms at Lade, had first to break the ice. And when he went to clear his lay-lines he found some of the fish frozen solid. March brought better weather and a resumption of air raids, but mainly at night and with London as the main target. Now, however, the skies were dominated by the RAF, our night-fighters destroying twenty-two enemy aircraft over the south-east.

In the first months of war many panic decisions had been made, but as resources became available and the threat of invasion lessened, organization improved, especially in Civil Defence. On the Marsh the Home Guard were at first part of the Ashford company under a Capt Swan, with a Romney Marsh platoon of four sections – Brenzett and Brookland, Dymchurch, Lydd, and New Romney. Because of the large number of recruits, the Ashford company became No. 1 Battalion, Kent Home Guard, with the four Marsh sections each being promoted to platoons with a Capt Brown as company commander.

The NAAFI van, a very welcome visitor to troops stationed in remote areas of the Marsh, is seen at Dengemarsh staffed by Miss Hilda Balcomb and Miss Doris Prebble.

In 1941 most units had weapons of some sort and training in their use was carried out at Lydd Camp. Platoons trained one night a week or had lectures and were expected to be on duty another night. Training with and against the Regular Army took place on several occasions, and Brenzett and Brookland liaised with any newly arrived troops in their area to help familiarize them with the many routes across the Marsh, showing them how to avoid the roads by using lookers' paths and bridges.

The Lydd platoon had first to improvise. With Charlie Elderkin as platoon officer and Ginger Pope as platoon sergeant, they drilled in Lydd school playground without uniforms or weapons, wearing LDV armbands. Their first guns were Canadian Ross rifles used during the First World War. Percy Clark, of New Romney, who joined the Home Guard and then became a leader in the Auxiliary Units recalls:

The water tower on Denge Beach which supplied the majority of Romney Marsh and was guarded at various times by units of the Home Guard. Close by, in 1944, were the oil pipes and installations of PLUTO, but fortunately the two liquids were kept separate.

We in the New Romney platoon had our headquarters in the hall at the Light Railway station, where the model exhibition is now. We had a firing range in the old mill yard, now part of Southlands School complex. Our first instruction was given by NCOs of the Somerset Light Infantry. Our commanding officer was the local Lloyds Bank manager, Mr Ray.

We had to guard certain places and patrol certain areas, the telephone exchange by the Methodist chapel, and also the water tower on Denge Beach. We only did these after dark. We went on at 10 p.m. until 6 a.m., taking it in turns to patrol. One night I had just got my head down when someone woke me and said 'There's people coming across the beach from the sea.' I went out and listened; it sounded just like a regiment of soldiers walking across the beach. It was, in fact, rabbits; hundreds of them scurrying about.

Maurice Addy, who joined the Lydd platoon as soon as he was old enough, rising to the rank of 2nd lieutenant, remembers:

Our first headquarters was in a house, Glenthorne, in Skinner Road, which was empty at the time. But as more joined we moved to the Baptist chapel in Ness Road. But that, too, became too small, so we then went to the old drill hall, now called the Institute, in Station Road.

At first there were no weapons, then we had old First World War rifles. We got quite excited at one stage when Thompson sub-machine guns arrived. But we had hardly unpacked them when we were told it was a mistake and they wanted them back. We then received the Browning light automatic; it held eighteen rounds and could fire single or rapid.

Later one of the other weapons I remember was the Northover Projector. This consisted of a metal tube, with a Heath Robinson firing mechanism which you could open and charge with explosive, and down the barrel we would slide a bottle of phosphorus. This was used as an anti-tank weapon. Once fired we had to run to the front and swab the barrel with water. If you didn't, the next bottle would explode in the barrel. Dreadful stuff. We practised with this weapon on the beach at Galloways.

For grenade-throwing we went to Littlestone golf course, where they had a range. Another time we were taken to Camber Sands, where we had to crawl through the sand dunes towards officers of the Regular Army while they fired over our heads with live ammunition. It was to give us some idea what being fired at sounded like. You could hear the crack. The same day we crawled along the shoreline and they fired just above us with Bren guns.

Mike Allen remembers joining a cadet force, the idea being that when you reached the age to join the Home Guard you would be semi-trained. Many young people volunteered, but not perhaps for the right reasons. 'Of course all the lads joined, mainly because at the drill hall they ran a canteen. It was managed by George Cullen, assisted by his wife Grace.

A section of Lydd Home Guard, 1942. Back row, left to right: Tom Stickells, -?-; middle row: John Linford, Ron Smithers, Jim Noakes, Alf Manning, Ted Cooper, Bill Sims, Mick Broad, Ray Button, Nelson Batchelor; seated: Cyril Reeves, George Cullen, Albert Flisher, Charlie Elderkin, Jack Pope, Reg Browning and Reg Adams.

When we joined, the officer, Mr Elderkin, signed the back of our identity card so that we could use the canteen to buy chocolate and sweets off ration.' The cadet scheme was soon abandoned. Maybe they ran out of chocolate! Meanwhile, military training continued. Thousands of troops from all parts of the Commonwealth came to Lydd to use the ranges and many others trained on the outskirts of towns and villages.

Enemy air activity in March was mostly concentrated on bombing inland targets, especially the London area. During a Marsh air battle on 12 March a Spitfire crashed at Old Romney, killing the pilot, Flt Sgt Glendenning. On 19 March eight Me109s came in over New Romney, dropped several bombs at Lympne, then went out low over Hythe, machine-gunning the town as they went. One, however, was brought down in the Channel by our fighters. The same day, and on 20 March, the skies throbbed with enemy planes passing over on their way to London.

At Lydd Council meeting on 23 March the councillors agreed to buy new equipment for the town's fire brigade: 12 × 35 ft rung ladders, 12 × 25 ft rung ladders, 36 buckets, 12 shovels and 12 stirrup pumps. They also placed an order with Hobson & Sons, London, for eight firemen's tunics and the same number of pairs of trousers, the tunics costing 42s each and the trousers 22s. It was proposed that the 1890 Merryweather fire engine be advertised for sale, but following the intervention of ex-fire chief Mr H.J. Blacklocks, supported by the Mayor, Mr G.T. Paine, it was decided to keep it. (Today the engine has pride of place in Lydd Museum.)

The RAF had a bad day on 16 March, with four fighter aircraft crashing on the Marsh. A Polish pilot, Boguslaw Mierzwa, flying with 303 Squadron, was escorting six Blenheim bombers when they were attacked over the Channel off Dungeness by several Me109s. His crippled Spitfire nose-dived with a terrific noise into the shingle near the old school. Local schoolchildren erected a small cross at the site but there is no trace left today. In the same dogfight a Hurricane crash-landed near the Light Railway bridge on the Dymchurch–New Romney road; its pilot, G.A.L. Manton, was unhurt. Another Hurricane was shot down at Newchurch, the pilot baling out and landing at Dymchurch, and the pilot of a Spitfire escaped injury when his aircraft crash-landed at Lade. Many British bombers crossed to France during the night of 19 April, while German aircraft passed over the Marsh on their way to drop bombs inland. The dark sky was aglow with fires on the French coast and the glare of the exploding enemy bombs silhouetted the line of the hills to the north-west. On 22 April eight Me109s came along the coast from the east, machine-gunning on the way.

Unlike the present day, in the war years there were plenty of fish in the sea, particularly in the West Bay. The difficulty for the fishermen was a curfew banning them from going to sea except from daylight to dusk. Another obstacle was the restricted zone in front of Lydd Ranges that stretched several miles out to sea and from which all vessels were banned when firing was in progress. This fanned the flame of animosity between the Navy and the Army, although if a naval convoy came in close the guns were silenced – provided the Army had been notified in advance. On a clear day in April, Dengemarsh fisherman Steve Prebble and his brother Tom were fishing well outside the zone when they noticed two frigates entering it. Steve recalls: 'We watched these two and several shells exploded very close to them. They turned smartly and went out to sea. You can imagine the

A group of landgirls from the Lydd hostel at a fundraising event at The Grange, Lydd, on 13 May 1941.

Admiralty took great exception to this. And two days later several naval ships entered the zone, before firing commenced, and anchored, and they remained for several days so that the Army couldn't fire. We used to wonder sometimes if they realized that a war was on.'

Air-raid sirens sounded early on 28 April as enemy planes clashed with RAF fighters in the skies over the Marsh. The pilot of an ME109 was lost when his plane came down in the Channel, but the pilot of a Hurricane that crashed at Kemps Hill, between New Romney and Lydd, lived to fly another day.

On 1 May the government issued figures to show how successful recruiting for the Women's Land Army had been since it was reborn in June 1939 – a similar army had been formed during the First World War. Although there were few landgirls on the Marsh in 1940, in 1941 three hostels had to be built to cope with them all, one at Kitewell Lane, Lydd, another at Brenzett and a third at St Mary in the Marsh. The Lydd and Brenzett buildings still stand. District welfare officer for the landgirls was Miss Anne Roper, of Littlestone. Grace Hawks, now Grace Elvy, who came to Lydd in 1941 after spending two months as a landgirl on Mr Stickell's farm at Newchurch, remembers:

I joined the Land Army at Wrotham. I travelled with another girl, Gwen Boxhall, down to Romney Marsh, and coming down by train from Ashford we wondered what we had let ourselves in for because the land was so flat and open. After two months at Newchurch we were moved to the hostel at Lydd. It was like a large dormitory, with bunk beds on either side. There were about six baths, each in a small cubicle with a washbasin. When we finished work it was pandemonium, with everyone wanting a bath before dinner.

When we first arrived the food was awful; the sandwiches we had for lunchtime could usually be seen floating in the dykes – minus the jam, of course. Gwen and I decided to buy our own sandwiches from the Methodist chapel, which ran a canteen in the evening. We went there most nights for a natter and to write our letters. The food at the hostel improved with the arrival of a new cook, Mary King, who came from Appledore. She was the sister of the butcher at Brookland, Sam Coleman. She turned out to be a smashing cook.

After our meal one evening, which was usually about 6 p.m., the matron came in and told us that nobody was allowed out; we were all confined to the hostel until further notice. Two of the girls had head lice. We had to wash our hair in Oil of Sassafras, after which we took turns at combing each other's hair over spread newspapers and watched out for lice. Because of this we had to miss the dances held at Lydd Camp. An officer came to ask why the girls were missing the dances. Matron hoped he had not seen the bottle of Sassafras.

When we were there, there were twenty-four girls at the hostel. We worked on Saturday mornings, and if we wanted time off we had to make it up in the evenings. If an air raid occurred while we were in the fields there was nowhere to hide, so you just crouched down and pulled your cape over you for a bit of camouflage.

Gwen Boxhall, the friend Grace Hawks met through the Land Army, came from Goodwood, in West Sussex. She says:

I travelled by train from Chichester to London and met up with several girls on my way to Harrietsham, where we were to work. We were billeted at Chapman's Farm. It was not until I was sent to Newchurch that I met Grace, and after a while we were sent to the hostel at Lydd. We were detailed to work for Mr Gordon Paine, in a gang of ten, mainly doing hoeing. Our chargehand was a local girl called Milly Reeves. We started at 7.30 a.m., an hour for dinner, and finished at 4.30 p.m.; on Saturdays till noon. The Land Army supplied dungarees, Airtex shirts and pullovers, and for going out, as they called it, corduroy breeches, socks and shoes. Later we were given an overcoat and a hat.

On 3 May a Blenheim Mk IV bomber from Manston, hit by enemy fire while crossing the Channel, crashed into the sea some 20 miles from Dungeness. Although a thorough search was carried out no survivors were found. The crew of three were named as Flt Sgts Deane, Chell and Watkinson. While fishermen Dick Tart and Bob Scholl were in the West Bay on 26 May an Me109 ditched close to their boat, the pilot making sure, perhaps, that he would be rescued. They brought him ashore at Galloways and handed him over to the military.

New ration books became available for collection in May, to be used from 1 July. The local paper of 7 June carried the story of a young Lydd lad confined to a hospital bed in Sevenoaks with a hip disease. Throughout a period of nearly two years he had had to endure callipers on his left leg and his right leg strapped high to the bedpost. Even so, the lad, Donald Harmer, son of Mr and Mrs E. Harmer, was doing his bit for the war effort. During his time in hospital he had saved enough from his pocket money to buy twenty savings certificates. Born in Australia, and proud of his countrymen and their achievements in the Middle East, he said that in the next war he hoped to be an Anzac!

A German pilot managed to bale out and land safely near Warren House, New Romney, on 8 June, his crippled plane plunging into the sea. Two other enemy aircraft crashed the same day, one near the water tower on Denge Beach and the other at Dengemarsh. All three pilots were taken prisoner. At Lydd Police Court on 18 June Herbert Fulljames of Maidstone and Harry Ballingtyne of St Leonards were each fined £2 for being on Romney Marsh without a permit – a continuing problem for the police, but made easier by the fact that any stranger, after the incidents with the spies, was treated with great suspicion and generally reported.

The New Romney Civic Restaurant was officially opened on 21 June by Mrs W.P. Spens, wife of the MP for Ashford and the Marsh area. She thanked the Romney Marsh Women's Voluntary Service for doing such sterling work to make it a great success. A total of 100 dinners were served, with music played throughout by a military band. Later that evening Marsh residents turned out to watch four large formations of bombers, escorted by many fighters, crossing overhead on their way to targets in France.

A merchant convoy proceeding up the Channel on 4 July came under heavy attack off Dungeness by German fighters, which were eventually driven off by Spitfires and Hurricanes. Seven days later another convoy was fired on by the big guns on the French coast, two of the shells being reported as having landed on the beach.

Old Bill was blown up when he stepped on a landmine at Dengemarsh on 13 July; a great loss to Mrs Nell Prebble, for he was her only billy goat. Three months later her favourite nanny goat, Sandy McNab, suffered a similar fate. Lydd Town Council, on 14 July, gave permission for the Home Guard to hold a charity dance at the Guild Hall – provided the dancers did not wear hobnailed boots. Also, to help the 'Grow for Victory' campaign, they agreed to let the townspeople have allotments free of charge for the duration. Miss Peggy Prince, awarded the OBE in 1940 for rescuing a British airman from the sea, was fined £2 at Dymchurch Police Court on 16 July for being on the sands at Dymchurch without a permit. On the same day Frederick and Violet Blacke, of Hope All Saints, and Edward James Greenstreet were also ordered to pay £2 each for being in a restricted area at Littlestone.

France was again the target for British bombers on 21 July, when large formations passed over the Marsh. One of the escorting Spitfires developed engine trouble and made a forced landing on the sands at Greatstone.

August got off to a wet start, delaying the much-needed harvest, and without the help of the landgirls and the many local women doing farm work the yield would have been poor. The contribution made by the Marsh women to the war effort on the land is sometimes overlooked, yet many drove horses or tractors and some were responsible for training landgirls.

On 18 August the National Fire Service came into being; instead of local councils running their own brigades they now all came under central control, with Mr Marshall Bott, MBE, ex-chief constable of Dover, being responsible for the Marsh area. In the early evening of the same day a Blenheim MkIV from Manston, hit by enemy fire over France, struggled back as far as East Guldeford, where it crashed. The pilot, Flt Sgt Stevens, was killed; the other two

Members of the Lydd Fire Brigade, which had become part of the National Fire Service, with their Dennis engine, 1942. Left to right: Joe Munds, Ernie Frampton, Tom Else, Reg Browning, Dick Greenstreet, Rob Wellstead and Capt Fred Baker.

crew members, Flt Sgts Vickers and Lowe, were injured and taken to Rye Hospital. Long-range guns at Cap Gris-Nez shelled a British convoy in the Channel for nearly an hour on 20 August. Some of the shells sent up great columns of water as they pitched near the shore and a few actually reached dry land – one nearly to the outskirts of Lydd.

To enter the Marsh from the hinterland, access had to be via bridges over the Military Canal. Some of these were demolished; others had demolition charges attached in case of invasion. On 5 September, at 9 a.m., someone or something caused the Appledore bridge to blow up, rocking the village and causing damage but no serious casualties. Within a few days the bridge was rebuilt by No. 3 Section, 501 Field Company, Royal Engineers. It is still in use today.

On 22 September, at 8.20 p.m., a motor launch on patrol just off Littlestone hit a breakaway mine and was wrecked. The menace of rogue mines continued to plague the local fishermen, the lifeboat crews and service personnel. It became the norm that fishermen hauling in their nets looked first not at the catch of fish but to make sure they had not caught a mine. On several occasions net and catch had to be abandoned. Compensation could be claimed for the net but not for the lost fish. Steve Prebble met the naval salvage officer who had come to inspect the wreck of the *Roseburn* at Dengemarsh:

I asked him if he tied the mines with 'spun yarn'. He said the trouble with mines in the Strait of Dover was that most of our merchant ships were abroad when war broke out and minefields were laid in haste with hardly any records kept. So to safeguard our own ships they were fitted with paravanes, an invention from the First World War. This

Miss Denton's house in Lyndhurst Road, Dymchurch, after a direct hit by an enemy bomb, 24 September 1941.

apparatus consisted of wires from the bow, with buoy-like kites to hold them away from the ship, and if the ship entered a mine area the mines would slide along the wire until they came to the kite, where a cutter would set the mine adrift.

I remember one afternoon shortly afterwards a large mine, one of ours, came ashore at Dengemarsh. A sentry was posted to guard it, only a young lad. Well, in the early hours of the following morning we were woken by a huge explosion, the beach stones rattling everywhere. Our first thoughts were for the poor fellow. I pulled on some clothes and ran towards the spot, and this sentry came running towards me shouting, 'It's gone off, it's gone off.' The poor chap was in shock and had gone deaf, but he had had a very lucky escape.

The Army gave assistance of a different sort on 13 October when they supported local talent at a very successful concert organized by Mrs Gordon Finn-Kelcey in New Romney church hall. Patron Lady Reading made a visit to New Romney on 22 October to see the work being carried out by the local branch of the WVS. She met members in the Civic Restaurant and congratulated them not only on their achievements but also on their spirit in working in such a precarious area.

A Whitley V bomber, returning from a raid on Nuremberg on 15 October, ran out of fuel and crashed near Hythe, but the crew all baled out safely. Almost a month later, on 10 November, the ack-ack guns fortunately stayed silent when an unfamiliar aircraft came in off the sea near Jury's Gap, flew low along the coast over Lydd Ranges and Dengemarsh, and then crash-landed near the Britannia Inn at Dungeness. It was a German commercial aircraft and its crew, two young Frenchmen, had stolen it to fly to Britain to join the Free French forces.

Pax House, Dymchurch, was used by the RAF as a recreation centre. Unbeknown to those playing billiards there one evening, a delayed action bomb had fallen nearby earlier. It exploded shortly after the last airmen had left the house.

On Wednesday 3 December a mystery death occurred, which is still debated in Lydd even today. Mr George Andrew Franks, a 55-year-old builder, of Coronation Square, was found lying unconscious at the foot of the stairs in the unoccupied Rectory in Dennes Lane, and died later in hospital at Ashford. The Rector, Canon Collins, had moved to Bexhill because of failing health, and Mr Franks had gone to the Rectory to check the lagging on the water pipes. When he had not returned by midday his wife asked employee Mr Albert Shepherd, of Ice House, Manor Road, to go and look for him. At the subsequent Lydd inquest Mr Shepherd said: 'I found Mr Franks lying at the bottom of the stairway; he was bleeding from a wound on the back of his head. The floor was tiled and dry, so I don't think he could have slipped. There was a doorway at the bottom of the stairs where he was lying and it was open. The doorway at the top of the stairs was shut.'

Sgt J. Tye of Lydd Police stated: 'I went to the Rectory after receiving a telephone message in the early afternoon of 3 December. I entered by the back door and went through another door into a passage. There was a small pool of blood 7 in from the stair wall and about 4 in from a harmonium. I opened the stair door and went up the stairs. There were eight stairs on the first half, then a small platform and six more stairs. At the top was a door which was closed. The top half of the stairs was very dark, but at the position the deceased was lying it seems very unlikely to me that he had fallen down the stairs.' The coroner, summing up, said: 'On the evidence before me it is not possible to find how the deceased came to fall. My verdict can only be that the deceased was found on the floor of the Rectory, Lydd, with a fracture of the skull, there being no evidence to show how the injury was caused.'

Mr Franks was a well-known and respected tradesman. There was much speculation as to how he had met his death. Most people thought he had disturbed an intruder and because of the capture of spies the previous year German agents were regarded as the main suspects. Later the same month two farm labourers, George Bourner and Duggie Apps, were cycling to work when they spotted a man in the Rectory gateway who quickly vanished into the shrubbery. The previous September a rubber dinghy had been found, half hidden, on the coast between Dungeness and Dengemarsh. Police kept it under surveillance for several days and it was eventually removed by an RAF unit.

The Rectory at Lydd, now known as The Glebe, the scene of Mr Franks's mysterious death in 1941.

When New Romney School closed for the Christmas holiday on 19 December it was announced that when it reopened in January there would be only four classes because evacuation had reduced the number of pupils so significantly. The headteacher, Mrs W.M.G. Hodges, would take one class and Mrs G. Foreman, Miss E. Thomas and Miss N. Wacher the remaining three. The children could be supplied with a cheap dinner from the new Civic Restaurant. The bakehouse at Lydd was also offering a useful service – to bake residents' home-made Christmas cakes for a fee of sixpence each. Mrs Dorothy Coleman, pushing her baby son in his pram, took her cake there. But no sooner had she arrived than a fierce air battle developed overhead. So while the adults at the bakehouse crouched under the tables, the baby was put in one of the ovens for safety. Not one of those in use, of course!

NINE

1942

January and February 1942 were relatively quiet months, the only big bang being caused by a dog setting off a landmine. March, however, began with a fierce exchange of fire when German warplanes attacked a convoy coming up-Channel on the first day of the month. On most late afternoons large formations of Wellingtons, Whitleys, Manchesters, Stirlings and Halifaxes passed overhead *en route* for raids on French factories producing military supplies for Germany. On 9 March a Hurricane escorting Wellingtons and Stirlings on a raid on Le Havre crashed at Brenzett and was burnt out.

On 1 April enemy planes attacking Dover and Folkestone were chased down the coast and jettisoned their bombs at St Mary's Bay and Dengemarsh before turning out to sea. On 24 April the area was rocked by explosions when a herd of bullocks got into a minefield at Greatstone. Sheep caused a similar blast in the same village on 26 April and several buildings were damaged. Earlier the same day Lydd Camp was again the target of a German raid, with many casualties and a number of buildings damaged. The Royal Naval Signal Station and the Coastguard lookout at Dungeness were machine-gunned.

The enemy stepped up their attacks in May. On the 5th four Me109s appeared out of the sea mist over Dymchurch and, flying at about 200 ft, dropped several bombs and machine-gunned at will. One woman was killed and several people were injured. Three days later Me109s again struck at Dymchurch and Hythe as well, inflicting many casualties. On 10 March, in a similar lightning raid, one civilian, a Mr Dixon of New Romney, and six soldiers were killed when bombs fell on the Sands Hotel at St Mary's Bay. Five of the soldiers – Sgt W.J. Goodridge and Gunners T.W. Coats, H. Hugill, H.J. Edwards and E. Blundell – were from 258 Battery, Royal Artillery, based at the hotel. The sixth was Pte S.T. Edes of the 2nd Battalion, 5th Leicester Regiment.

A Wellington bomber returning from a raid on Boulogne on 18 May ditched in the sea off Littlestone due to engine failure, but its crew of five – Sqn Ldr Laird, Plt Off Leeson, and Flt Sgts Inman, Blackenridge and Moses – came ashore in their rubber dinghy. The plane was later blown up by set charges. On 22 May a Spitfire, hit during an air battle, crashed into the sea off Dymchurch, the pilot being rescued by an RAF launch. On most evenings British bombers, with fighter escort, crossed the Channel in large numbers, and when the weather was clear fires as well as gun flashes could be seen along the French coast. On 31 May the body of Uffz G. Heinz, whose Ju88 had plunged into the sea off Winchelsea earlier in the month, was retrieved off Dungeness.

British bombers continued their missions in June, with the Germans now and then retaliating. In a raid on 18 June bombs fell at Snargate and military installations were machine-gunned at Dungeness, with a few minor casualties. The next day bullets fired in air battles damaged several houses at Littlestone. A week later. during the early hours of 26 June a Wellington returning from a raid on Bremen made a forced landing near Lower Agney Farm, Scotney, Lydd. The pilot, Sgt P.C. Teall, made his way to Red House Farm, Scotney to use the telephone. He told Mr and Mrs Charlie Southerden and their daughter Nancy that he and his crew had been apprehensive until he heard looker George Wilson shouting to his sheepdogs to 'shut up'. George's son Les remembers:

> It was about four in the morning when we heard the crash, it came down about 300 yd from the house, and some of the crew came to our house. They believed they were in Holland. They had planned to set the aircraft on fire. It had come down in a green field after catching the top of a line of trees and came to rest with its nose just through a fence in a field of potatoes. In the summer months, sheep tend to sleep bunched up, and the plane landed on a group of sheep, killing many of them. All the crew were okay, but shaken. The aircraft was put on a low loader trailer and taken away. It was not too badly damaged.

Letters from the War Office were received by Lydd and New Romney Town Councils allowing shrimping to be resumed along certain stretches of the coastline to contribute to food supplies, and permits for lugworm digging were also made available. On 26 July Dymchurch was invaded – not by the enemy but by a huge cloud of Large White butterflies which flew in a long line towards Dungeness. The same day an Fw190 was shot down in the sea during a dogfight, the pilot, Lt F. Kruger, being rescued by an RAF launch. At the end of July the Marsh said goodbye to the men of the Sherwood Foresters who, during their tour of duty, had shared in the good and the bad times, and were to be remembered for their help and their kindness. Their place was taken by the Welsh Fusiliers.

On the last day of the month a damaged Spitfire, with engines on full throttle, came screaming over Lydd at roof-top height and hit the ground near Caldicot Crossing. The pilot was seriously injured. Another Spitfire, hit during an engagement over Occupied France, crash-landed near the railway gatehouse in Church Lane, New Romney. Farmer Ernie Prior, his son Gordon, Derek Frew and Leonard Reynolds, who were working in fields nearby, carried the pilot, Sqn Ldr Kennard, to the first-aid post in New Romney, from where he was later taken to hospital.

The harvest of 1942 was a critical factor in the outcome of the war, and it changed the farming scene on Romney Marsh. Pastures disappeared as land was ploughed for the first time since the land was won from the sea, and work began on the wettest areas to produce the well-drained Marsh we have today. Extra arable and extra yields meant more labour. The Women's Land Army had already closed the gaps left by conscripted farmhands and local women were a tremendous asset. Additional labour was needed at harvest time and farmer Dick Body at Snargate found another source: 'Soldiers stationed in the area were glad to come and work on our farm in their off-duty time. A private's pay was 2s a day; less if married as there was a deduction towards his wife's separation allowance. A Royal Artillery unit was stationed at Appledore for quite some while, and particularly helpful was a company of Leicesters waiting for the Allied invasion of North Africa, where incidentally they suffered heavy losses helping the Americans.'

Every member of a farming family had to help in some way. Audrey Hammond (née Cobb), a schoolgirl and farmer's daughter of Millbank Farm in the parish of Ruckinge, reminisces:

> It was hard going to get the harvest in. We had no combine harvester; sheaves of corn, mostly wheat and oats, were loaded on to wagons, twelve loads of sheaves to each stack. The stacks could be placed in pairs but there was a minimum distance that the next stack had to be built in case of fire from incendiary bombs or other sources. These stacks were all thatched with straw from last year's harvest.
>
> For haymaking, harvesting and threshing, it was possible to get extra rations by filling in special forms and taking them to the local Food Ministry office. As many family members as possible would be included in the working number. Mother would purchase the extra rations, keeping tea and sugar, as she made the drink at the usual three break times in the working day. The rations of cheese, jam, margarine or butter would go to each person listed.

Landgirls Grace Hawks and Gwen Boxall were moved from the Lydd hostel to live and work on Mr Newton's farm at Brookland. Here they were joined by another landgirl, Betty Clark, from Yorkshire, who also had two sisters in the Land Army based on the Marsh. Gwen Boxall much preferred living away from the hostel:

> All three of us were billeted at Harvey Farm. It was much better; we lived in as a family and were more free. The hostel was full of rules and regulations. We went to the farm mainly to work with the thresher; when we were not required for this, we did other jobs: cutting beans – a hard job – and also picking up potatoes. We worked side by side with the men. We got on all right; they showed us the best way to do jobs. Working with us was Ron Newton, who later became my husband. There was also an old character we called 'Swedey' living in a caravan. I believe his proper name was Alfred Wood. Mr Newton Sr drove the steam engine and we travelled with it all over the Marsh. We were paid by the Land Army, about £1 7s 6d for a 48-hour week.

Because there were no facilities at Harvey Farm, the three girls went down into Brookland village on a Friday night to Mr and Mrs G. Pope's for a bath. The cost was sixpence and they took it in turns, as they had to share the same water. Harvey Farm had also only an outside privy at the bottom of the garden, and Grace remembers the embarrassment and amusement this caused: 'It had an old-fashioned wooden seat, one large hole and one small. If the wind was blowing and it was in a certain direction, when you used your small square of newspaper it would blow up the other hole, for the toilet was open at the back.'

On 8 August fleeing enemy aircraft, chased by our fighters, unloaded their bombs over Greatstone and Lade. Houses were damaged but no serious injuries were incurred. One of the German planes, a Ju88, crashed 8 miles south of Dungeness; its crew of four,

Taking a welcome break from threshing, workers at the Newton's farm at Brookland, 1941. Left to right: Landgirls Gwen Boxhall, Betty Clark and Grace Hawkes with two of the farm hands.

Obfw H. Hadderhorst and Obergefrs K. Buchur, J. Bauer and K. Schmitt, were missing. In a night raid on 11 August incendiary bombs fell between Jesson and Burmarsh, causing considerable damage to corn crops. Incendiaries were also dropped at Scotney, Lydd, hitting Red House, the home of Mr and Mrs Charlie Southerden and their daughter Nancy. Nancy, now Mrs Armstrong, remembers:

Because of the closeness of the dropping bombs, my parents and I got up and dressed and went into the air-raid shelter, the first time we had done this. When the aircraft had gone, my father went outside to see what damage there was and to check on the horse and the milking cow. I went to the shelter entrance and shouted to my father that our house had been hit and was on fire. The fire had started in the loft, where the fleeces of wool were stored until sold to the wool company. We managed to rescue many of our belongings before it became no longer safe to enter the building. I think the funniest thing, looking back on it now, was when I realized that the only footwear I had were the rubber boots I was wearing. My dad said he would get my shoe rack, which was under my bedroom window. He was very reluctant to break the window; then he realised the house was being burnt to the ground anyway, so he went ahead, smashed the window and saved my rack and six pairs of decent shoes.

Four Fw190s swept in almost at sea level between Dengemarsh and Galloways on 1 September, their target being Lydd Camp. Bombs were seen leaving the aircraft, one scoring a direct hit on the military hospital, killing one soldier and injuring several others. Five more soldiers died as bombs wrecked other buildings, and three workers were killed and many more injured by a bomb which fell on the Galloways road, under construction at the time. All the injured were taken to the British Legion Hut before being ferried to various hospitals and some large hotels in Folkestone, which were used as casualty units. While returning to his unit at Dungeness from leave on 4 September, using the Romney, Hythe and Dymchurch Light Railway, which had been taken over by the War Office in 1940, Gnr Joseph Forbes was killed instantly when he leaned out of a carriage window and struck his head on a bridge.

On 16 September two Rye fishermen, Messrs Hollands and Longley, were killed when their fishing boat *Mizpah* was machine-gunned as it left Rye Harbour for the fishing grounds. The skipper, Mr Locke, was injured. A severe explosion from the French coast at 10.40 p.m. on 19 September was the result of a raid by a large force of British bombers that had crossed the Marsh minutes earlier. It was announced at this time that Lydd had had 2,002 air-raid warnings since the war began and New Romney, 2,000.

On 22 September there were more fatalities at Rye when bombs dropped on Cinque Ports Street destroyed the cinema and badly damaged the Cinque Ports Hotel. Another bomb fell in the Strand area and a third in the vicinity of the Ypres Tower. Four people were killed and many injured. No sirens sounded at Dymchurch on the 24th because enemy bombs had brought down the power lines. Frequently raiders were overhead before any warning was given. Two people were killed when a single bomb dropped in Tram Road, Rye Harbour, on the afternoon of 7 October. Several more bombs fell at Winchelsea Beach. After they had endured enemy raids and endless practice firing by British troops since the war began, the Prebble families at Dengemarsh and the Freathys at Galloways were finally given the order from the War Office to move into Lydd.

Unfortunately, accidents sometimes occurred. On Thursday 22 October, during a fierce air battle, an RAF Beaufort was brought down by British guns and crashed near Rye. More bombs fell at Littlestone on the 25th, damaging Pope's Hotel and other properties. One of the most remarkable incidents of the war on the Marsh took place on 27 November when an Fw190 was brought down by a train! Two Fws had flown in very low, machine-gunning various targets, before spotting the 3.15 p.m. leaving Lydd station. The train, carrying some sixty passengers, mostly service personnel, was approaching Caldicot Crossing on its way towards Brookland when one of the planes made a low head-on attack, machine-gunning as it came. The second plane followed suit and it is thought that its cannon shells struck the locomotive boiler, which exploded. Fragments from it hit the aircraft as it turned away and blew it up. The RAF report claimed the plane clipped the locomotive's steam dome, and of the few eye-witnesses there were some who refuted this, while others agreed. The pilot, Oberfw H. Bierwirth, was found dead in a dyke some distance away. None of the train passengers was seriously hurt. The fireman, Mr W.D. Hills, suffered scalds on his arms, but the driver, Mr C. Gilbert of Ashford, escaped unharmed. The first Fw190 had meanwhile begun machine-gunning Lydd, the only casualty being Mr R. Tart, of Tarts Cottages in Skinner Road, who was in his garden and was hit in the leg by a cannon shell. Of the train drama, Jack Carpenter, a police messenger boy, recollects:

The boiler of this locomotive, photographed at Lydd station on 27 November 1942, exploded and brought down an Fw190 which was attacking it.

I was in Lydd police station; the sirens had sounded a few minutes earlier. I heard the 3.15 p.m. train leave the station, so I wandered outside towards the railway bridge. I then heard machine-gun fire, so I ran to the bottom of the bridge and, as I looked up, a fighter plane was just swerving away on the Romney side of the track. I then saw the other one, and from where I was there was a cloud of smoke and steam. Then, as the plane appeared over it, there was a large fireball, and the plane seemed to disintegrate. The plane's engine was a ball of flame; it seemed to take off and sail over towards the Rectory, some quarter of a mile away. I ran back to the police station and told them what had happened. At the same time the phone rang reporting it. Sgt Tye told me to go to Westbroke and report to PC Thatcher. Mr Thatcher was waiting for me; he told me to go and see if my father wanted help, my father being PC Carpenter, who had been checking the sheep-dipping at Westbroke when it happened.

I found my father at the scene. Looking along the track I saw the locomotive, which appeared to consist only of the platform and cab. People were still being helped from the carriages. My father then said 'What we've got to do is look for the pilot', so Len Prebble and I went into one field and my father into the other, on the Lydd side of the railway track. We followed the dik along and spotted an open parachute. I shouted to my father, 'Here's the parachute.' We started hauling in the parachute and pulled out the dead pilot. All his pores were red. Whether this was caused by the explosion, I don't know, but he didn't stand a chance at that low altitude. We laid his body on the bank and covered it with the parachute.

The locomotive was repaired and returned to service in 1943.

On 29 November a posthumous Victoria Cross was won by the pilot of an RAF Stirling I bomber which crashed into the sea off Dymchurch at 2.15 a.m. on its way back from a raid on Turin. The aircraft had been hit several times while over its target, one shell exploding in the cockpit, injuring both pilots and the wireless operator. The skipper, Flt Sgt R. Middleton, was temporarily knocked unconscious, but his co-pilot, Flt Sgt L. Hyder, managed to position the plane and the bombs were released. Twice more the Stirling was hit on its return journey and Flt Sgt Middleton, seriously wounded, realized there was little chance of landing the plane safely. As he approached Dymchurch he flew parallel with the coast and ordered two crew to bale out. Before they could all escape the plane hit the sea, killing Middleton, Flt Sgt J. Jeffery and Flt Sgt J. Mackie. The other five crew members survived: Plt Off N. Skinner and Flt Sgts Gough and L. Hyder suffering injuries, but Flt Sgts G. Royde and D. Cameron escaped unharmed.

Lydd was attacked on 22 December, bombs falling on the Rype and on the outskirts of the town. However, the two days of Christmas passed peacefully with no raids or alerts, although British aircraft still passed over, even during Christmas Day, on bombing raids on enemy arms factories.

On the civilian front in 1942, the people of the Marsh raised £28,000 during Warship Week for the purchase of a trawler-minesweeper christened HMS *Romney*. To celebrate, a big parade was held in New Romney, led by the Band of the Royal Marines, followed by contingents of soldiers and marines with bayonets fixed, ambulances, the fire brigades of

Pam Adams (at the wheel) and Mrs Ford with a car converted into an ambulance, in the grounds of Elm Grove, Lydd, which became the Ambulance Brigade HQ in 1942.

A mile of books! This was the target for the schoolchildren of Lydd – because of an acute paper shortage as many books as possible were collected for recycling. Mrs Frank Austin supervises the local children laying books along the kerbstones at the west end of Lydd, almost completing the target.

Lydd, Romney, Dymchurch and Brenzett, ARP units, Home Guards, Scouts and Guides, with Bren-gun carriers bringing up the rear. The salute was taken by a senior Army officer and local dignitaries. Lydd also exceeded its target of raising £6,000 towards the cost of a tank, the Local War Savings Committee sending the War Office a cheque for £6,584.

Lydd's WVS did its bit for the war effort by producing 140 knitted items, including 56 pairs of socks, for the Army, Navy and Italian prisoners of war, as well as making boys' knickers (40 pairs), girls' underwear (42 garments) and 40 frocks and cardigans for homeless families, and 12 hot-water-bottle covers for local distribution.

Dances were held most weekends in all the towns and villages in the area. These were a good way of raising money for the war effort, and also helped to raise the spirits of both locals and troops in these rather dark times. Those too young to attend listened with great envy to the music and general pleasantry when doors and windows were left open.

TEN

ADVANCE LANDING GROUNDS

In 1941 more fighter airfields were required in south-east England to tackle enemy bombers and fighter-bombers. It was necessary to provide cover for Allied bombers in their daylight missions over the Continent and to give air support to troops when the day came for the invasion of Europe. A search was made for suitable sites for ALGs – advance landing grounds. Because of its flat, open landscape, Romney Marsh was considered ideal and Brenzett, Newchurch, St Mary-in-the-Marsh and Midley were selected as sites on which to build four airfields.

The work began in 1942 and was largely undertaken by 503 Works Squadron, which was based mainly in Nissen huts at Brenzett. But the weather was atrocious – very heavy rain, sleet and a biting east wind which lasted for weeks. Faced with a sea of mud, as well as damp and cold accommodation, the men called for better conditions. Their pleas were ignored, so they downed tools and troops had to be brought in from Lydd to maintain discipline. However, eventually, the service chiefs listened to the demands, promises were made and the men resumed work. Shortly afterwards 503 Squadron was transferred to Ringmer, in Sussex, and 42 Squadron, which took its place, was formed by recruiting men from a number of squadrons, presumably on the principle of divide and conquer. The accommodation problem was solved by moving the men to requisitioned houses at St Mary's Bay and trucking them to work each day.

The chosen airfield sites were all on farmland, so dykes were piped and filled in, minor roads closed or diverted and farm houses requisitioned or demolished. Then, once the land was levelled, Somerfield track (very heavy gauge wire mesh) was laid and pegged down with long ½ in steel rods driven into the ground. In the wetter areas coconut matting provided an 'underlay'. Runways were all 50 ft wide but their length varied. Because camouflaging these airfields was difficult, the runways and perimeter tracks were sown with a variety of grasses, of differing shades of green, giving the appearance from the air of a series of small fields. The seed was obtained from seed merchants East and Loud Ltd of Ashford. The grass had to be kept short, so at Midley sheep were grazed on the runways, with looker Bert Huggett close at hand with his dogs to fetch off the sheep at take-off or landing.

One of the servicemen drafted into 42 Squadron was George Frampton, who later married a local girl, Molly Lancaster, and after the war settled down on the Marsh. He recalls:

The 503 Squadron had a problem and we, 42 Squadron, took over. I travelled down from Essex, entering the Marsh for the very first time. I thought I had come to the last place on earth. We were put to work at Newchurch. What a mess that place was in; all

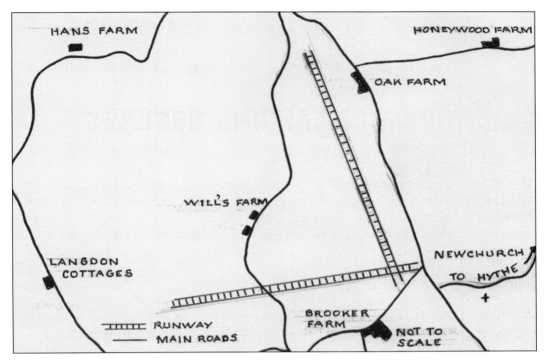

Map of the Advance Landing Ground, Newchurch. Drawn by Patricia L. Higgins.

roads were covered in 4 in of mud and you couldn't walk properly anywhere without the risk of slipping over. I don't know how the local people put up with it. But as the summer progressed the mud dried out and it became a pleasant place to work in. The runway had already been constructed and all we had to do was the outer perimeter and the roads.

Each airstrip eventually had four blisterhangars, as well as armoury, petrol and oil points, cookhouse and stores, fire tender and motor transport, air-raid shelters and sleeping quarters, the latter sometimes being augmented by tents. For headquarters Nissen huts were used at Midley, Brooks Farm at Newchurch, Honeychild Manor at St Mary-in-the-Marsh and Moat House at Brenzett. The airfields were closed for the winter because of flooding; the Marsh was not as well drained as it is today.

Midley was the first airfield to become operational, with 245 Squadron moving in on 30 June 1943, flying Typhoons. Newchurch and St Mary-in-the-Marsh opened on 2 July of the same year, 19 Squadron with Spitfires and 182 Squadron with Typhoons respectively. Finally, on 14 September, 122 Squadron took over Brenzett with Spitfires. The busiest time for these airfields was in 1944, when they were used extensively during the D-Day landings. A wing of rocket-firing Hurricanes remained at Newchurch, using Will's Farm as their base. George Frampton watched their coming and going: 'They used

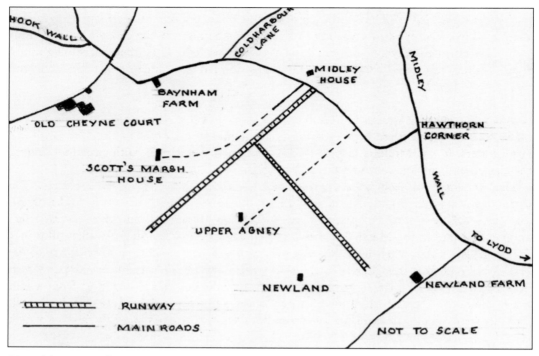

Map of the ALG, Midley. Drawn by Patricia L. Higgins.

to go out in twos and threes, but I do remember six setting off at one time. Their targets were railways, trains, stations and bridges. They also carried synchronized cameras, and good photographs of rockets heading towards trains and of trains blowing up were lying about at Will's Farm for all to see. I went back to work there several years later, and when the field beside Will's Farm was being ploughed, the plough hit something hard. It turned out to be a load of live rockets.'

The most important role played by the Marsh airfields was in the fight against the Doodlebugs – the flying bombs – which began crossing the area in large numbers from June 1944. Not only did the Marsh aircrews have to bring them down without blowing themselves up; they had also to dodge the fire from British ack-ack guns which were blasting off at them. Wg Cdr Beaumont and his aircrews at Newchurch accounted for 670 Doodlebugs, and the Polish wing at Brenzett also claimed a considerable bag.

The airfields themselves did not escape enemy action, being bombed on several occasions. George Frampton remembers one such incident at Newchurch on 24 March 1943:

We first saw this squadron of Fw190s come in over Dymchurch heading for Ashford, where they did considerable damage. They returned over Bilsington, and right before them was the Newchurch runway, with 240 blokes repairing the Somerfield track and tensioning it. From where I was I could see the turf kicking up as the cannon shells rained down. They didn't hit a single man on the runway but one fellow jumped into the dyke and was nearly drowned. The aircraft sheered off over the Bull Inn, firing as they went and knocking the chimney off. They then machine-gunned the church and killed sheep in the field beyond. The marks can still be seen on the church today.

A few days after this attack six 500 lb bombs were dropped on the airfield runways and many tons of rubble were brought from bomb-damaged buildings in London to fill the large craters. It was Midley's turn to be attacked on 15 September, with casualties among the airmen and damage to runways and buildings.

The airfields had a chequered career, what with crashes and forced landings. The Typhoons got off to a bad start at St Mary-in-the-Marsh. One crashed after take-off on 26 July 1943; two more collided over the airfield on 15 August; and the very next day another St Mary-in-the-Marsh Typhoon crashed at Dengemarsh. An Australian pilot in a Typhoon was killed when he failed to clear some tall trees on Snave Corner, along the Ivychurch road. It is thought he was blinded by leaking Glycol after his aircraft had been badly damaged in combat. On 6 September a Marauder returning in trouble from a raid crash-landed on the airfield and burnt out. Only a few hours later three of the Marsh airfields were a welcome sight for seventeen bombers – Fortresses and Liberators – which

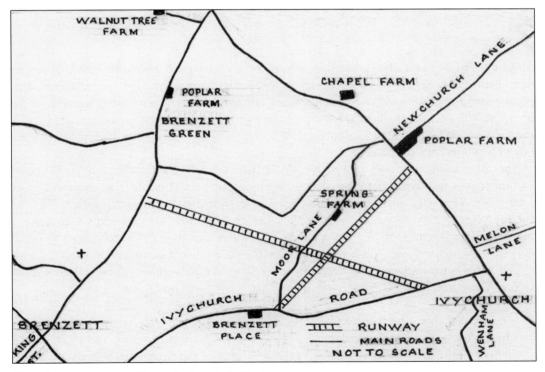

Map of the ALG, Brenzett. Drawn by Patricia L. Higgins.

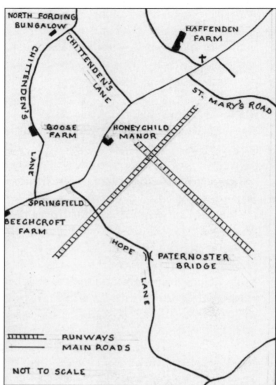

This Typhoon ran out of runway while making an emergency landing at St Mary-in-the-Marsh in summer 1944. The pilot, Jeff Hadley of 181 Squadron, escaped injury.

Map of the ALG, St Mary-in-the-Marsh. Drawn by Patricia L. Higgins.

made emergency landings, short of fuel, after raids deep into Germany. Those that landed at St Mary-in-the-Marsh did so safely, but at Newchurch one overshot the runway and came to rest partly on the Bilsington road, while another made a perfect landing in a cornfield at Willow Farm and had to be dismantled. The only mishap at Midley was when a bomber overshot and ended up with its nose on the road close to Midley Poorhouses. At Brenzett a Fortress made a forced landing on its belly, with its nose up against the hedge opposite New Home Farm at Brenzett Green.

The Marsh airfields were evacuated for the winter on 5 October 1943, but a Liberator in trouble crash-landed at St Mary-in-the-Marsh on 30 December. The plane was wrecked but its crew of ten escaped injury. Two Hurricanes collided at Newchurch in 1943, although the exact date is not known. George Frampton recalls: 'The Hurricanes came in, in squadron formation, four arms of three to peel off, to the right and left, and the centre one goes up and comes back over, then they land in formation, following one another in. What happened that day we never found out, but the one in the centre and the one on the left collided, and both came down near Mill Bank Farm. I believe one pilot was killed and the other seriously injured.'

The only visible reminder of the airfield at Midley is this Nissen hut that stands opposite Midley Poorhouses.

On 5 July 1944 a Marauder landed safely at St Mary-in-the-Marsh on one engine. A crewman was seen to bale out over Lade Sands but his parachute failed to open. Another Marauder, with its port engine dead, also put down safely at the same airfield on 12 July, and a Liberator, short of fuel, landed there on 17 July. Two days later a Fortress landed at Midley on one engine; on 25 July a Liberator crash-landed at St Mary-in-the-Marsh but the crew were unharmed; and on 29 July another Liberator made an emergency landing at the same airfield.

The Marsh airfields have now been long returned to agriculture and few signs remain of their wartime role: a Nissen hut alongside the road at Midley, a U-shaped concrete road near Hawthorn Corner where the air-raid and sleeping shelters were, and bits of Somerfield tracking used to reinforce hedges at Newchurch and St Mary-in-the-Marsh. But Spitfires and Messerschmitts still fly in the Midley area, for the Romney Marsh Model Flying Club has its flying base there. And not far away is the Brenzett Aeronautical Museum with lots of relics from the war years. The table overleaf lists the squadrons that served on the Advance Landing Grounds at Romney Marsh.

BRENZETT

No. 122 Squadron	14–16 September 1943	Spitfires
No. 129 Squadron	9 July – 10 October 1944	Spitfires
No. 306 Squadron	9 July – 10 October 1944	Spitfires
No. 315 Squadron	10 July – 10 October 1944	Mustangs

NEWCHURCH

No. 19 Squadron	2 July – 18 August 1943	Spitfires
No. 132 Squadron	2 July – 12 October 1943	Spitfires
No. 602 Squadron	13 August – 12 October 1943	Spitfires
No. 184 Squadron	18 August – 12 October 1943	Hurricanes
No. 56 Squadron	28 April – 23 September 1944	Spitfires and Tempests
No. 3 Squadron	28 April – 21 September 1944	Tempests

ST MARY-IN-THE-MARSH

No. 182 Squadron	2 July – 22 September 1943	Typhoons
No. 181 Squadron	10 July – 13 August 1944	Typhoons
No. 247 Squadron	10 July – 13 August 1944	Typhoons

MIDLEY

No. 245 Squadron	30 June – 10 October 1943	Typhoons
No. 175 Squadron	1 July – 9 October 1944	Typhoons
No. 174 Squadron	1 July – 10 October 1944	Typhoons

ELEVEN

1943

Although German air raids continued sporadically over Romney Marsh in 1943 there was the heartening sight and sound of Allied bombers heading out over the Channel night after night and, increasingly, by day. The enemy was now on the receiving end. And the British successes in North Africa (leading to the surrender of Italy), the German defeats in Russia, and the big build-up in Britain in preparation for D-Day at last generated a real feeling of optimism.

Food, beer and tobacco were still in short supply, and with more troops on the Marsh complaints were made that some shopkeepers were selling them provisions. An order had been issued in 1942 forbidding this practice, the military and Police were reminded, and warning notices were distributed.

Bad weather over Britain and Europe caused flooding problems for farmers on the Marsh in early January and kept the Luftwaffe grounded. The first incident of the month occurred on 17 January when a guncrew failed to recognize a British plane and brought down a Hurricane; the pilot managed to bale out safely at Hammonds Corner, near New Romney. His aircraft crashed on the outskirts of Lydd, setting off two landmines. Late that afternoon a Beaufighter plunged into the sea after being hit over France, one of the crew managing to bale out just in time and landing at Newlands, Midley. And in the evening an enemy aircraft dropped bombs at Northfording, St Mary-in-the-Marsh, but they failed to explode.

Early the following day German planes returning to France jettisoned bombs which fell close to Honeychild Manor, St Mary-in-the-

NOTICE

The Regional Commissioner for the No. 12 (South Eastern) Region calls attention to the following South Eastern **Army Orders which have been issued to Military Formations.**

Purchase of Food and Tobacco by Troops on the March.

Cases have arisen of troops on the march being halted in a village and allowed to fall out and purchase food in the village shops, with the result that no food was available for the inhabitants later.

In cases of this sort, the Army, which is provided with adequate rations, and has suitable further provision made in the canteens run by the N.A.A.F.I., is buying and consuming the limited supplies available for the civilian population.

Such conduct is not only a breach of discipline, but is also calculated to damage the good feeling which should exist between the Army and the civilian population.

When on the march or in convoy, troops are forbidden to fall out for the purpose of entering the shops of any town or village in which the column may be halted.

MONSELL.

Regional Commissioner for the No. 12 (South Eastern) Region.

BREDBURY,
TUNBRIDGE WELLS.
10th June, 1942.

For distribution to all retailers for information and display on their premises.

A pamphlet, issued in June 1942, that forbids troops from purchasing food in local shops.

Marsh; they also failed to go off. It was announced the same day that Sgt Walter Thomas Upton, of Dymchurch, serving with No. 61 Squadron, had been awarded the Distinguished Flying Medal. The remainder of January was dominated in the air by large formations of our bombers, with fighter escort, passing morning and evening to attack targets in Occupied France and Germany. The body of Uffz H. Bremer, whose Fw190 had been shot down by ack-ack fire over Rye Bay on 1 January, was found on the shoreline at Littlestone.

On 4 February, failure to hear an order saved the life of one crew member of a Stirling bomber damaged during a raid on Nuremberg. When the pilot had to put down in the sea east of Dungeness he told his crew to bale out. Flt Sgt D.R. Sparton did not hear the order, and when he eventually baled out the wind carried him inland to Snargate. The remainder of the crew landed in the sea and were drowned. Dungeness lifeboat launched immediately permission was given and, with Coxswain Doug Oiller aboard, searched the area for six hours, finding only wreckage and oil on the water. Those lost were WOII W. Freeland and Sgt L. Toupin, Royal Canadian Air Force, Flt Sgt R. Thorne and Sgts G. Bell, J. Goddard and H. Kilvington.

Education was a disruptive affair for those Marsh children who had not been evacuated. Directly the sirens sounded they headed for air-raid shelters; the Brenzett pupils spent nearly all day in their bunker on 8 March. At New Romney the school shelter had no seating, no heating, leaked badly when it rained hard and was prone to flooding, so the children had to crouch under their desks or in a coalshed. Eventually improvements were made, but one teacher, Mrs Anne Holdstock, noticed during a raid that one little boy looked very worried. Asked what was the matter, he replied: 'It's Dad. He'll never get those taters in if this goes on.'

On 13 March a number of New Romney men who cycled to work at Lydd Camp were caught riding without lights. PC Cooper of Lydd gave evidence and the men were fined 5s per light. A Dymchurch villager in a similar incident insisted that he had had a light. The policeman demanded 'Are you calling me a liar?' The diplomatic reply was: 'Well, let's put it this way: if anyone else was to call you a liar I wouldn't disagree.' The war had its lighter side, including a review put on by the Guides and Scouts of Lydd in aid of the Prisoners of War Fund, at the Drill Hall in Station Road on 26 March. Staged by J. Pearman, D. Haydon, D. Bensted and H. Cryer, the show included music by Mrs F. Rowe and B. Fagg, on accordions. Those who took part were Isobel Stanley, Margaret Turner, Jean and Kathleen Stickells, Avril Piper, Dennis Adams, Rita Fagg, Jean Jones, Joan Baker, Sheila Gillett and Doreen Godfrey. A considerable sum was raised.

Prompt action by an observant auxiliary coastguard at his lookout at Jury's Gap in the early hours of 31 March resulted in all but three of the twenty-one crew of a naval trawler being rescued in a strong south-west gale. At 1.50 a.m. John Southerden, peering into darkness and hampered by heavy rain, saw what he thought to be a white flare for a brief moment about a mile and a half away. He contacted Lade Coastguard Station and Fairlight, requesting lifeboats. At 2.13 a.m. he spotted a vessel at 180° sounding her siren and firing Very lights. John Southerden assembled the Jury's Gap life-saving team and all available coastguards and auxiliaries. Men of the nearby No. 415 Battery, Royal Artillery, joined in. Station Officer Harding, who took command, said:

I fired the first rocket at approximately 0235 hours; it fell short of the vessel. Six more rockets were fired but, because of the weather, all fell short. The state of the weather was 6 to 7, sea 5, deteriorating all the while. About 0400 hours men were observed leaving the vessel using a raft. I sent patrols along the beach with lifelines. At approximately 0500 hours fourteen men had managed to gain the shore 1 mile eastward, and these were assisted by the patrol.

One man who had apparently drowned was given artificial respiration and treatment for restoration by me and he recovered sufficiently to be assisted to the observation post, where he received attention. Another man washed ashore 1½ miles eastward was pulled from the water by Auxiliary Coastguard Southerden, and he and Lt Bell of 415 Battery gave artificial respiration, but he failed to recover.

My district officer arrived at 0415 hours and he sent an Army lorry to Lydd for the Galloways life-saving crew, who arrived at 0543. Lydd police and Lydd doctors R. and E. Palmer attended to the survivors. The vessel was the *Caulonia*, a Navy trawler.

The Dungeness lifeboat had been alerted at 2.10 a.m. and the Hastings one at 2.16 a.m. But permission to launch had to be given by the Admiralty, Dover, and in the case of Dungeness it was not given until 3.20 a.m. Several times Coxswain Oiller rang Dover. His daughter Doris remembers her father slamming the receiver down so hard she thought the telephone was going to break. The Hastings lifeboat had been given the go-ahead, but the launch was prolonged and arduous. A strong west-south-west gale was blowing, with very heavy rain, and a big ground swell was breaking a quarter of a mile offshore. Contractors had been working on new coastal defences, and obstacles from these, strewn across the

The crew of the Hastings lifeboat Cyril and Lilian Bishop, *which rescued the crew of the minesweeper* Caulonia *in extreme weather conditions, 31 March 1943.*

Members of the crew of the Dungeness lifeboat Charles Cooper Henderson, *who served with the lifeboat in those dark and dangerous years of the Second World War.*

launching area by the rough sea, had to be removed. After many attempts, and aided by civilians and troops, the *Cyril and Lilian Bishop* got afloat at 4.30 a.m. and reached the *Caulonia* at about 5.30 a.m., just as dawn was breaking.

The sea had now moderated slightly and the trawler lay well inside broken water, broadside on to the seas, with only her mast, funnel and bridge showing. Seven survivors were clinging to the bridge. With great determination Coxswain John Muggridge brought the lifeboat close enough, despite heavy seas and floating wreckage, to pass a line and the seven men were all able to scramble to safety. The Dungeness lifeboat was finally allowed to launch at 4.20 a.m. and ordered to proceed at utmost speed to Jury's Gap. Coxswain Oiller's log states: 'We did this as quickly as possible and approached the casualty. We found the Hastings lifeboat in attendance, rescuing the remaining survivors. We stood by until they were all rescued. On our return journey to our station we saw a tank landing-barge drifting 4 miles east of Dungeness. We went out to see if there was anyone aboard but found no-one. We arrived at our station at 8.30 a.m.'

Of the twenty-one men aboard the *Caulonia* three were lost. The survivors owed their lives to the vigilance of John Southerden, and to the rescue efforts of the coastguards and auxiliaries, the officers and men of No. 415 Battery and to the lifeboatmen. The lifeboat crews that day were: Hastings: Coxswain J. Muggridge, 2nd Coxswain E. Adams, Mechanic W. Hilder,

The remains of the wrecked Caulonia *off Jury's Gap, East Sussex. The marker pole was swept away in a gale in 1997 and has not yet been replaced.*

2nd Mechanic W. Martin, Bowman F. White and crewmen R. Harffey, C. Haster, G. Mitchell and W. Harffey; Dungeness: Coxswain D. Oiller, 2nd Coxswain J. Oiller, Mechanic A.J. Oiller, 2nd Mechanic A.P. Oiller, Bowman F. Oiller and crewmen J.W. Oiller, G. Tart, A. Haines, J. Brignall and W. Brignall. Coxswain Muggridge and Mechanic Hilder of the Hastings lifeboat were both awarded RNLI bronze medals for their part in the rescue, and the other crew members received the institution's thanks on vellum, as well as cash awards. Sadly, neither Coxswain Muggridge nor Mechanic Hilder lived to receive their medals – the former was killed when his fishing boat was blown up by a mine on 10 April and the latter died when a bomb fell on the Swan Inn, High Street, Hastings, on 23 May. A marker buoy was visible on the *Caulonia* at Jury's Gap until 1997, when it was swept away in a south-west gale.

Between 1 and 8 May the Marsh did its bit for 'Wings for Victory Week'. New Romney with Dymchurch, and the villages in Romney Marsh proper, set a target of £20,000 to provide a Catalina flying-boat. The week began in New Romney with a parade of troops, civilian organizations and schoolchildren, an address being given by the local MP, Mr E.P. Smith, and the salute being taken by Sqn Ldr Martin Thompson. The Mayor, Alderman C. Cavey, began a mile of pennies from the town hall. Along with dances, whist drives, darts matches and fêtes in the villages, the festivities raised a grand total of £25,000 – enough for a Catalina and a Spitfire. At Lydd and Dungeness, where a target was set of £10,000 for two Spitfires, the activities began with a parade, starting in Coronation Square and being led round the streets by a military band. The small community of Dungeness set its own contribution at £2,000, exceeding it, with hard work, by £825. Altogether £32,178 17s 6d was raised, which was enough for six Spitfires.

A 'Wings for Victory Week' pamphlet, which details the amount it was hoped to raise in Lydd and Dungeness.

A War Office inspector, touring the Marsh to check whether air-raid shelters issued to the public were being used for their proper purpose, found a Morrison shelter being used as a farm chicken-house and quite a number being used as workbenches for all manner of purposes, including making coffins. Pigs, sheepdogs, ducks, potatoes and apples were being kept in Anderson shelters, and on one isolated farm a shelter had replaced the garden privy. All these misuses merited a fine but no time could be found to bring prosecutions.

On 22 June three Messerschmitt 109s returning from a raid on Ashford and heading back to France jettisoned their bombs before they left the coast and a number of sheep were killed by a bomb which fell in a field at Turngates Bridge, St Mary-in-the-Marsh. The following month, on 24 July, when a landmine exploded close to their gun battery in the dunes at Greatstone a number of soldiers had to be treated for ear damage and shock. The area had been declared safe, but the problem with mine clearance was that no records were kept of where and how many mines had been laid. On the same day a party of Royal Engineers making a pathway to the sea through a minefield at Dungeness accidentally detonated a complete string of mines, causing many minor injuries, mainly due to falling stones, and damage to property.

A story of exceptional heroism lay behind the crash-landing of a Lancaster at Snave just after 3 a.m. on 1 September. The aircraft, of 106 Squadron, Syerston, Nottingham, was hit by flak while taking part in a big raid on Berlin. The pilot, Flt Off H.D. Ham, lost a foot and also suffered severe arm injuries. Two of the Lancaster's engines were damaged.

Although in agony from his wounds, Flt Off Ham ordered his crew to strap him to his seat; then he nursed the aircraft back across Europe. In crash-landing at Wey Street, Snave, a wing clipped and demolished one end of a bungalow, Elmhurst, then struck some willows and burst into flames. The bungalow's occupier, Miss Sweatman, was unhurt and fetched buckets of water to help quell the fire, saying afterwards that she was more concerned with the safety of the lads on board than her own plight.

Six of the crew survived. Unfortunately one of them, wireless operator Sgt J.W. Weight, was badly injured and died next day in Willesborough Hospital. Rear gunner Sgt T. Waller was less seriously hurt. Not until daybreak did the searchers find the body of Flg Off Ham. His supreme courage and fortitude had saved the lives of five of his crew. In addition to Sgt Waller the five were: flight engineer Sgt N. Gale, navigator Flg Off C. Pitman, bomb aimer Sgt J.E. Jones and middle gunner Flt Sgt N.D. Higman.

Although the four Marsh advance landing grounds were principally used by fighters, many aircraft, especially bombers, made for them when in trouble – as happened on 6 September. A squadron of American Flying Fortresses of the 9th Tactical Air Force, returning from raids on Germany, had been so harassed by enemy fighters and guns, and had had to make so many detours, that they were short of fuel. Three landed at St Mary's and five at Midley, one ended up on the Brookland road, one crash-landed beside the Dymchurch road just outside New Romney, while another, most of whose crew had baled out, crash-landed at Jury's Gap.

On 17 September the body of a 26-year-old American airman, Flt Sgt Walter F. Migut, of No. 91 Bomber Group, was recovered from the sea at Dymchurch. Also on the same day a Beaufighter of No. 29 Squadron shot down a Ju88 near King Street Crossing at Brenzett. The German crew of four, Oberfz F. Funk, Uffz K. Sailer, Uffz J. Fleishchman and Uffz J. Binder were killed on impact. A lone German aircraft dropped bombs in a line from Greatstone to Dengemarsh on 21 October, but several failed to explode. However, because they were so close to the railway line, trains were held up until they had been dealt with. The following day an unfamiliar aircraft, a Lockheed Lightning, was seen escorting a large formation of American Marauders, and on 31 October sixteen Mosquitoes flew low over New Romney on their way to bomb the Ruhr Valley and the port of Emden.

A German Junkers 88 was shot down in the sea south of Dungeness on 5 November, all three of its crew – Lt Bernhard, Fw K. Kohler and Fw Eurers – losing their lives. On the 6th E-boats attacked a convoy as it passed Dungeness Point but were driven off, the destroyer *Whigshed* hitting three of them and sinking one. A British aircraft dropped nine incendiary bombs on the beach at Dungeness, very close to the Pilot Inn, on 18 November; it was a bright moonlit night but apparently not bright enough! On 25 November a lone enemy aircraft dropped bombs on land at Goose Farm, St Mary-in-the-Marsh, and at Melon Farm, Ivychurch; more bombs were dropped at Dymchurch and Dungeness as German planes slipped back across the Channel; and two German overload fuel tanks fell behind Ellis's timber yard at New Romney.

A Hurricane plunged on to the beach at Dungeness on 3 December after the pilot had baled out, and on the 10th the body of American airman Sgt Mitchell D. Miles of 509 Bomber Squadron was washed ashore at St Mary's Bay. An enemy plane returning to France on 11 December was brought down by ack-ack fire and crashed near Rye, its

Lydd, Dungeness and Greatstone "Salute the Soldier Week"
PROGRAMME FOR THE WEEK

SATURDAY, MAY 27th.
2 p.m.—Selections by a Band of *The Buffs* in Coronation Square.
2.30—Official Opening by Brigadier O. P. Edgcumbe, C.B E., M.C.
3 to 3.30—Band will beat Retreat in Coronation Square.
4 to 5.30—Exhibition at The School, of Military Equipment and Schoolchildren's Posters and Slogans.
6.30—Parade with Band starting from New Street, and proceeding via. Bond's Corner, Station Road, High Street, Tile Hall and Park Street to Coronation Square where the Salute will be taken by Brigadier O. P. Edgcumbe, and Parade dismissed.
8.00—Grand Salute the Soldier Dance, at the Camp Gymnasium. Military Dance Band. Tickets 1/6; Ladies & H.M. Forces, 1/-.

WHIT SUNDAY.
6.30—Special Salute the Soldier Service at the Old Parish Church.

WHIT MONDAY.
6.0 to 7 o—Exhibition at the School.
8.0 to 11.0—Lydd Home Guard Carnival Dance. Admission 1/6.

TUESDAY, 30th.
Lloyd's Bank will open especially for Salute the Soldier Week, from 10 a.m. to 2 p.m.
6.0 to 8.0 p.m.—Magnificent Exhibition of Guns, Models, Training Rooms, also an extensive Range of Photographs depicting the North African and Italian Campaigns, Air Offensives and Naval scenes. Entrance Free at Camp Main Gate.

WEDNESDAY, 31st.
3.30—Garden Fête at The Grange, Lydd (entrance opposite "Star") including Baby Show, at 4.0 open to Lydd and Dungeness babies. Up to 3 months; 3 months to 1 year; 1 to 2 years. Fancy Dress Parade, Decorated Cycles, Prams, etc. at 6.0, numerous Side-shows and Displays, Light Refreshments and Teas. Watch for details.

THURSDAY, JUNE 1st.
7.0—Mobile Cinema Van at The Pilot, Dungeness. Special Speaker. Films, including one featuring General Montgomery.
6.0 to 8.0—Last chance to see this wonderful Exhibition (*see Tuesday*)

FRIDAY, 2nd.
3.30 to 4.30 and 6.0 to 7.0—Mobile Cinema Van in Coronation Square.
7.30—Grand Salute the Soldier Whist Drive, at the Home Guard Drill Hall. Admission 1/3. Special Prizes.

SATURDAY, 3rd.
3.30 to 4.30 and 6.0 to 7.0—Mobile Cinema Van in Coronation Square.
7.0 to 11.0—Home Guard Salute the Soldier Dance at the Drill Hall.

Selling Centre open daily (excepting Wednesday, when Stamps and Certificates will be on sale at the Fête).
Display of Photographs and Lists of Lydd Serving Men and Women, at the Selling Centre. Please help to make these as complete as possible.
Darts Tournament at the Rising Sun. Entrance Fee 1/-.
Special Films at Lydd Cinema by courtesy of Mr. McCormack.
The public are asked to hang out Flags and Bunting to make the Town as bright as possible and so "Salute the Soldier."
BOOKS will be gratefully accepted at the Selling Centre for OUR SHIP H.M.S. LYDD.

The programme for 'Salute the Soldier Week', to be held at Lydd. The target, to raise £15,000 for five armoured cars, was exceeded and the final sum collected was £40,334.

bombs exploding on impact; there were no survivors. Also on this day three wartime policemen based at Lydd – PCs F. Jones, G. Cooper and J. Carpenter – were transferred to the Petroleum Warfare Department to work locally on PLUTO, the 'Pipeline Under The Ocean'. On 23 December there was an hour-long duel, beginning at 8.15 p.m., between long-range guns on both sides of the Channel.

Peace reigned over Christmas, with not a single air-raid warning, but on 30 December large numbers of British bombers flew over the Marsh in the early evening on their way to attack German cities. Later in the evening the crew of a Liberator had a lucky escape from death when the aircraft's fuselage snapped in two as it crash-landed at St Mary's landing ground. The Liberator, from 333 Bomber Squadron, stationed at Bury St Edmunds, was on a mission to bomb the Mannheim area of Germany, but after developing engine trouble had to turn back and was then attacked over France. After jettisoning his bombs, the pilot reduced height to 100 ft, then climbed to 2,000 ft as the coast was sighted and made for St Mary's because fuel was running low. On the last day of the year three Allied planes crashed on the Marsh: a Thunderbolt came down on the old railway line behind Lade, another, a Fortress, down near Jesson and one at Newchurch. There were no reports of any serious injuries.

TWELVE

PLUTO

Like the body of Sir John Moore at Corunna, at a critical time in another war in another place, they buried it 'darkly at dead of night . . . with their lanterns dimly burning'. What they buried was one of the Second World War's biggest secrets; the time was 1944 and the place, as described below, was the heart of Kent's Romney Marsh.

The secret's rather clumsy title, Pipeline Underwater Transport of Oil (later better known as Pipeline Under The Ocean), appropriately formed the acronym PLUTO, mythological god of the underworld, though probably a film cartoon animal was more readily recalled. It had all begun a year earlier, in 1942, when preliminary planning got underway for Operation Overlord, the massive counter invasion of Europe. Lord Mountbatten, then Chief of Combined Operations, conscious of the huge problem of keeping the Allied forces supplied with sufficient fuel for their drive towards Berlin, and of the sitting target that tankers and storage installations would present to the Luftwaffe, came up with the idea of laying a fuel pipeline across the English Channel.

The experts in this field showed little interest in the proposal, except for one man, Arthur Clifford Hartley, chief engineer of Anglo-Iranian Oil. It was his enthusiasm that got the project started, with a programme worked out under the direction of the Petroleum Warfare Department, employing units seconded from the Royal Navy and Army and roping in several civilian firms, notably Anglo-Iranian and Siemen Bros of Woolwich. Two years earlier, a fuel pipeline had been laid from Avonmouth to Walton-on-Thames to avoid tankers having to enter the English Channel to discharge. By 1942 Liverpool, the Isle of Grain in north Kent, Southampton and the large oil

Where the PLUTO pipe crossed the many Marsh dykes it was encased in concrete, which made excellent footbridges that largely remain today and help to identify the line of the pipe. This particular bridge is on the Brookland–Rye Harbour line.

After the war, many of the PLUTO sea pipes were recovered but some, such as this one at Lade, were missed and are sometimes exposed.

storage depot at Aldermaston had all plugged into it. Now it was decided that PLUTO would do likewise, and would be double-headed. One Channel crossing would be from the Isle of Wight to Cherbourg, code-named Bambi, the other from Dungeness to Boulogne – Dumbo!

By the end of 1943 a 70-mile supply line using 6 in and 8 in pipes had been laid from the eastern terminal at Walton-on-Thames to Dungeness. Following the railway tracks wherever possible – and certainly from Appledore to the coast – the work was mostly carried out at night, with a minimum of illumination, and great care was taken to replace turf and bushes to camouflage the pipeline. Even so, by D-Day part of the route was lined in red and yellow where poppies and charlock bloomed in the disturbed soil.

At Romney Marsh the main pipeline ran across Shirley Moor, near Woodchurch, into Appledore, forded the Military Canal on its bed close to the site of the modern sewage plant, ran over the Dowels, under the B2080 road and the Appledore–Rye railway line, and followed the Lydd rail track to the water tower at Dungeness. Many of the installations were concealed under and close to the huge piles of beach at the nearby quarry. This pipeline then divided in two, with one section going east to Lade and the other to specially constructed buildings near the lighthouse. There were two other branch lines – one from Brookland to Rye Harbour, the other from Lydd to Wye.

The branch from Brookland to Rye Harbour began from a junction near Brookland railway halt, ran north of Brookland village along to Pod Corner, through fields following the A259 road, across the field between the road and the Woolpack Inn and on to East Guldeford Corner. Here it again took to the fields via Colyer Farm, across the East Guldeford Level, west of the Rye golf course clubhouse, and into the Camber dunes and its rendezvous with thirteen big storage tanks. These and their pumps were roofed with clay to conceal them from the air, the clay having been imported because the wind kept blowing the sand away. A further two tanks were positioned nearer to the River Rother, with the pipeline continuing across the river bed to the railhead at Rye Harbour village. The branch from Lydd to Wye ran from a junction and pumping station in a field close to the rail bridge at Lydd and crossed under the line and the B2075 road to the land in front of Jaques Court. From there it followed the road, crossing Belgar Lane and continuing to the New Romney side of Hammonds Corner, across the A259, through the fields to Hope and on to St Mary-in-the-Marsh close to Beachcroft Farm. It then ran in almost a straight line to Newchurch, past Norwood Farm, through the village and on to Honeywood Farm, across the Military Canal to the west of Bonnington Church and again in an almost straight line to Wye.

Two types of cable were used for the Channel crossing; these were actually pipes but were called cables because the 3 in ones were made in similar fashion to hollow cable, and flexible so that they could be laid by a cable ship, and also because the name concealed their petrol-carrying function. The first, known as the Hais cable – after A.C. Hartley, Anglo-Iranian and Siemens, who co-operated in its manufacture – had to withstand a working pressure of over 1,000 psi. Some of the cabling was made in the USA.

The second cable, of 2 in and 3 in welded steel pipe, was called Hamel after its two creators, H.A. Hammich and B.J. Ellis. Made in 4,000 ft lengths, it was wound on to six huge drums, officially called conundrums but locally dubbed cotton reels. Each drum, which was 40 ft in diameter, was capable of carrying up to 80 miles of 3 in pipe weighing some 1,600 tons, and all were christened 'HMS Conundrum'. Some of the steel cable was brought to New Romney by Southern Railway and welded together in longer lengths on the platforms of the Romney, Hythe and Dymchurch Light Railway station. At first these lengths were transported to Dungeness by rail, but they proved too heavy for the track and had to be moved by road instead.

The Royal Navy's most powerful tugs, HMS *Buster* and HMS *Marauder* were given the task of towing the sixteen cables that were laid from Dungeness to Boulogne. A problem

Palmers House, Dungeness, which was requisitioned to contain part of the PLUTO installation. Many seaside homes were acquired for this purpose, some housed storage tanks, others pumps.

arose when bringing the cables ashore to connect them to the land system. Bob Gilham, then a young fisherman living at Lade, remembers going to watch. Two large ploughing engines were used to pull the pipes, but the pipes kept snapping due to the suction of the wet sands. In the end, the connections were welded on the sands and brought ashore by bulldozers.

Dungeness had been a restricted area since 1940. Now, during these secret operations, it became a demarcation zone, with armed sentries stationed to the east at Derville Road and on the coast road from Littlestone; to the west at the lighthouse; and to the north at the old railway crossing, now the entrance to the nuclear power stations. An Army officer visited every home, swearing the occupants to secrecy. All work was carried out at night. An 8 p.m. curfew, first imposed in 1940, was reintroduced and come daylight the night's work was already camouflaged and checked from a helicopter, nicknamed 'Camouflage Joe', which flew along the coast and the inland routes of the pipeline. One problem was the telltale tracks left in the shingle by vehicles and machines which were removed by using rollers, bundles of heavy netting, planks and logs towed by rubber-tyred tractors.

All the beach installations, storage tanks, heavy pumps and lengths of pipework had to be disguised. A few new buildings were erected, but mostly existing dwellings were adapted – a total of twenty-seven seaside bungalows and houses between Dungeness and Lade. A ringmain and a mass of pipes and pumps to propel the petrol across the Channel were sunk in the beach near the old fort. To camouflage this, Captain Lander, the chief camouflage officer, masterminded the construction of a large dome made of concrete and wire mesh, topped with pebbles. Its effectiveness was tested when a US airforce Lightning fighter made an emergency landing only a few yards away; the recovery crew who came to collect it were completely deceived.

The PLUTO bungalows, now being lived in, 1998. These houses look perfectly normal from the outside, but have extremely thick interior walls, reinforced to protect the pumps and tanks in case of a direct hit by enemy bombs.

Because of the high risk of a PLUTO fire at the Dungeness and Lade installations the National Fire Service permanently stationed a crew and engine at the coast, its members being drawn from various fire brigades.

The men working on PLUTO – which included the laying of the pipelines, construction of plant, conversion of private houses and bungalows, and operation of the system – were mainly from the Royal Engineers, Pioneer Corps, Royal Army Service Corps and Military Police. The officers' mess was at the Jolly Fisherman at Greatstone. The Royal Navy was mostly responsible for the sea cables, but many skilled civilians were employed and also trustworthy local men.

When the Channel cables were being laid to the storage tanks near the lighthouse a minefield had to be cleared. Mrs Ciss Tart, a fisherman's wife living at Dungeness, recalls: 'They planned to blow up a few of these mines at a time, and we would be warned when they began so that we could all get into our air-raid shelters and leave all our doors and windows open. I'd just done my springcleaning. I thought "I can't have all that dust come in" so I left mine all closed. What a mistake that was. We had a great deal of damage. The entire minefield had gone up. All our doors and windows were out and the ceilings down; all the fishing nets came down from the loft. Oh, what a mess.'

Once the petrol began to flow the great danger was that something might spark another type of explosion, so Dungeness was declared a 'no smoking' area, except for indoors, and a fire team, led by Officer Bill Dane, and based at Dungeness, was recruited from the National Fire Service. The hidden pipelines were walked daily by officials checking for leaks; they also made sure nothing had been built, dug or placed on them. The men carrying out this job had the authority to order anybody, including service personnel, to remove any obstructions. Fred Jones patrolled the line from Appledore to Dungeness. Once, near Brenzett, he found an Army unit camped too close to the line. He asked them

After breaking away from a convoy, this PLUTO conundrum was washed ashore at Greatstone. Maddieson's holiday camp is just visible on the left.

to move – but could not tell them the reason why. The captain in charge refused to move, so Fred produced his warrant and asked the officer to ring the telephone number on it. He returned 20 minutes later declaring that Fred must have friends in high places; he would move his troops immediately.

The line from Brookland to Rye Harbour was patrolled by Vic Dunster of Brenzett and the Lydd to Wye route by George Stredwick. Although the entire pipeline was policed, such was the secrecy that few of the patrolmen knew who their colleagues were. Other local men operated and maintained the security of the isolated inland pump houses.

There were many petrol leaks. But – in some cases thanks to luck – there were no fires. Early one morning, after a steam train had already passed over it on its way to New Romney, a large lake of petrol was discovered near the Lydd signal-box. Fortunately no hot coals had fallen from the engine's firebox. On another occasion a policeman checking on reports of incendiary bombs dropped at Lade found the bombs had failed to explode, but nearby he discovered a fountain of petrol. Residents took advantage of the leaks to augment their petrol ration, but there were few cars on the road at that time and the petrol was not much use as fishing-boat fuel. However, the fact that it leaked into some of the wells at Dungeness brought a piped water supply to the area.

After all this, did PLUTO play its expected vital role in the freeing of the Continent of its Nazi invaders? The answer has to be 'no'. The Isle of Wight to Cherbourg pipeline was almost a total failure. Pumping did not begin until 18 September 1944, far too late to be of any real use to the Allied forces, and the pipeline was abandoned on 4 October.

The giant conundrum ashore at Lade after losing its anchor in a gale in October 1944. The pipes can be clearly seen and its size can be gauged by the lady standing alongside.

Bob Gillham and his sister Margot pose on top of one of the PLUTO petrol storage tanks, 1944. These tanks' original position was at ground level with beach piled up around them, giving the appearance from the air of two large bomb craters. Other tanks were hidden inside houses.

Because of the absence of suitable brick buildings on Dungeness to house the large petrol tanks and the heavy pumps for the PLUTO project, buildings had to be erected. From the air these resembled the single-storey flat-roofed dwellings of the local area. Some of these buildings are seen here in 1981.

Attention was then concentrated on Dungeness, where laying of the sea cables began in October 1944 after the Boulogne approaches had been cleared of mines. But the weather deteriorated and the cable ships had to seek shelter in gales, which meant they then lost valuable fine days in resuming their positions. One giant conundrum broke loose and was stranded at Lade for several months. By the second week in December only six cables had been laid and their performance was disappointing, with only 700 tons of petrol crossing the Channel daily. During eighty-five days of operation up to 20 January 1945 the total reached only 62,000 tons. Other fuels were due to be supplied but never were, apart from some oil from the Isle of Grain. Things improved at Dungeness, with sixteen cables eventually being laid, and the pipeline was used daily until 30 July 1945, by which time it extended ashore as far as Frankfurt in Germany and Emmerigh in Holland.

Official figures show that by the end of the Second World War about 5.2 million tons of oil products had been delivered to the Continent, mainly through the ports. PLUTO's contribution was only 370,000 tons, less than 8 per cent. Nonetheless, it was a remarkable feat of design and engineering and one of the war's best-kept secrets.

THIRTEEN

1944

Although 1944 was a momentous year and, for the Allies, the real turning point of the war, for the people of the Marsh it began and ended with lots of action in the air. At first German bombs continued to be dropped and then came the menace of the Doodlebugs. On the very first day bombs fell at St Mary's Bay, but luckily mainly on the shore, while on the 2nd an Fw190, shot down by Mosquito pilot Flt Lt Heal, roared over Camber with its engine at full throttle, crashed on the sands and caught fire. The pilot was killed. On 15 January German planes on the way home dropped bombs at Lade and Midley, and four overload fuel tanks fell at New Romney.

On 21 January another shot-down Fw190 fell into the sea off Galloways and later the same day an Me410, hit by ack-ack fire, exploded on impact on the beach at Lydd Ranges. The bodies of the crew, Hptm K. Heintz and Fw O. Runge, were later buried at

The devastation caused by a US Fortress when it crashed in Lyndhurst Road, Dymchurch, 5 February 1944. A wing can be seen in the foreground, while the cockpit and fuselage lie further down on the left.

Folkestone. On 22 January a Dornier, cannon-shelled by a Mosquito of 488 Squadron, came down in the sea off Dungeness, while a second one, thought to have been brought down by the ack-ack gunners, ditched off Rye Harbour. Two airmen from the first plane, Uff W. Klune and W. Engelhardt, were picked up by RAF Air-Sea Rescue, but the other two crewmen were drowned. On the following day the body of F.W. Hirschfeld, killed in the Rye Harbour incident, was washed ashore at Galloways.

Allied bombing sorties continued unabated, day and night. During one, on 5 February, a Fortress from 96 Bomber Group, USAAF, developed engine trouble. The pilot jettisoned the bomb load and set course for England. Over the Channel the engine problem worsened and once over land he ordered the crew to bale out, then turned the plane's nose seawards before following suit. Unfortunately, the unmanned aircraft crashed in Lyndhurst Road, Dymchurch, where it demolished several bungalows and damaged many other buildings, including the police station. Pte Joseph Hampson of the 4th Battalion, Somerset Light Infantry, was killed and War Reserve Policeman Frank Woodland, his young son Derek and a friend, Ian Jones, who was playing with him, were injured. Many other people were lucky to escape.

There was a sour note at the February meeting of the New Romney Town Council when it was announced that an unknown person had extensively pilfered a consignment of fruit sent by the crew of the town's warship, HMS *Romney*. It was to have been divided among the local schoolchildren. The Mayor, Alderman C. Cavey, hoped those responsible for the theft were thoroughly ashamed of themselves.

Home-grown production of staple foods continued to be essential, thus freeing shipping to carry other vital cargoes. Unfortunately, increasing numbers of rats were helping themselves liberally to corn stored in stacks awaiting the arrival of the threshing machine.

The War Agriculture Executive had issued a Rats Order in 1942 under which farmers and threshing contractors had to surround stacks before threshing with wire-netting fences, not less than 30 in high, to prevent any rats escaping. The local boys and farm dogs then dealt with them. But there were also some pranks played, especially involving the Land Girls. Rae Harrington remembers working with the Blacklocks' threshing gang: 'Now and then they would play a trick on us, like one lunch time I put my jacket on and felt something soft in the pocket. When I pulled it out I had a handful of newborn rats, not a hair on them and nearly blue. Everyone fell about laughing when I screamed. It took me a long time to stop shaking.'

To tackle the worsening rat problem it had been decided to set up and train a Land Army anti-vermin squad. The two members sent to the Marsh in 1944 were former waitress Beryl Thomson, of Brenchley, near Tunbridge Wells, and former typist Jeanie Williams, from Maidstone. Only a short time previously they would both have jumped on a table at the sight of a mouse,

Rae Harrington 'models' the dress uniform of the Land Army minus the hat, which was never popular with the girls.

let alone a rat; now they travelled from farm to farm destroying sometimes as many as a hundred rats a day, and also giving training in the use of poisons and gassing and ferreting techniques to other Land Girls.

On 4 March a Typhoon involved in an air battle over the Marsh crashed near Greatstone station. The next day a Lockheed Lightning fell into the sea off Lade after a scrap with enemy fighters, the pilot being rescued by a Littlestone fishing boat crewed by Messrs J. Gates and S. Polhill.

That D-Day was round the corner was signalled on 21 March when the order already restricting the movement of civilians in the area was stepped up. This came into force on 1 April and covered the whole coast from the Wash to Penzance. For 'War Operations Reasons' the new order required permits for any movement within 10 miles of the sea, and these were only to be issued to people engaged in necessary business in the zone: people visiting parents, parents-in-law, or persons *in loco parentis*, or husbands and wives ordinarily resident there.

IMPORTANT NOTICE

Under directions given by the Regional Commissioner for the No. 12 (South Eastern) Region under Defence (General) Regulation 16A:—

1. No person other than a member of His Majesty's Forces or of a Police Force on duty shall between 10.30 p.m. and 8 a.m. or half-an-hour before sunrise (whichever time is earlier) be out of doors seawards of the boundary described below, except for the purpose of immediate and urgent necessity.

2. Any person out of doors between the said times for any such purpose of immediate and urgent necessity shall comply with any requirements for regulating his conduct while so out of doors which may be made by any member of His Majesty's Forces or of a Police Force on duty.

LOCAL GOVERNMENT AREA	BOUNDARY
Borough of Lydd	Southern Railway line to Lydd Town Station- Station Road-Harding Road - Robin Hood Lane - Camp Road - a line from the Roman Catholic Chapel to Road B2076 at West- broke House - Road B2076

A poster issued before D-Day forbidding visits to the coast.

As part of the rehearsal for D-Day there was practice-firing of heavy guns on Lydd Ranges; tanks and 'dukws' were tried out over concrete ramps – still visible today – built beside the Lydd–Camber road. Military exercises took place on Camber Sands, with troops being trained in the art of landing from assault craft. Rye Harbour was heavily guarded because of experiments there with amphibious tanks. Becoming known in the services as 'funnies', these tanks certainly looked peculiar with their long canvas sides. Naval vessels were using the harbour for repairs and refuelling, and many – including the Germans – thought the Allied invasion would be launched from this area because of its proximity to France and the increased military activity.

On 13 April an American Flying Fortress piloted by Lt W.H. Johnson lifted off from Rattlesden, Suffolk, to take part in a bombing raid on the Messerschmitt factories at Augsburg, Germany. But across the other side of the Channel the aircraft came under heavy anti-aircraft fire, and with several of the crew wounded and two engines out of action, Lt Johnson was forced to turn back. Although the bombs and all loose items were jettisoned, the aircraft lost height rapidly. Then another engine failed. As the Fortress crossed the coastline between Hythe and Dymchurch, Lt Johnson gave the order to bale out, but courageously stayed at the controls to give his nine crew members the chance to do this. Sadly, he himself was killed as the plane ploughed into the ground. For his bravery and self-sacrifice Lt Johnson was posthumously awarded the DSC, and in April 1997 a

D-Day ramps. As part of the rehearsal for the D-Day landings, several concrete structures were built at Lydd Camp for troops to practise loading and unloading vehicles onto boats and 'dukws'.

Soldiers pose with their 28-ton Cromwell tank after completing their D-Day training. Thousands of soldiers passed through Lydd Camp during the war, in addition to the permanent regiments defending the Marsh and surrounding district.

plaque was erected close to the spot where he died and the road was renamed Johnson's Corner. The members of his crew were: Lts H.H. Whiteley, W. Fancher and G. Nye, and Sgts F. Hazzard, J. Higgins, P. Simpson, E. Williams, K.L. Zeiger and P. Barkus.

Air battles continued to be fought over the Marsh. On 19 April a Ju188 bomber was shot down by a Mosquito night fighter of 85 Squadron and crashed in Melon Lane, Ivychurch. Two of the crew, Uffa W. Haberland and Gofr K. Leidecker, baled out and were taken prisoner, but the remaining three, Fw Helmutt Richter, Oberlt Albert Hein and Uffz Johannes Kohler, all in their twenties, were killed. Also killed, on 21 April, were the pilots of two Thunderbolts that collided over New Romney. But the crew of three from a crippled Marauder parachuted to safety at New Romney while their plane plunged into the sea. Not so lucky were all the crew of another Marauder who lost their lives when their machine ditched off Dymchurch on 30 April. Dungeness

A memorial plaque at Hamstreet to US airman Lt Johnson, who was killed when his B-17 crashed in the area on 13 April 1944.

lifeboat and rescue launches carried out an early morning search off Hythe on 1 May following reports that a Marauder had crashed into the sea, but only oil patches and wreckage were found.

Local hero Sqn Ldr Learoyd, VC was back on the Marsh on 13 May to open New Romney's 'Salute the Soldier Week'. This fundraising week aimed to raise £22,500 – the cost of ten 25-pounder guns – and actually collected £31,645 15s 2d. At Lydd a similar fundraising effort, called 'A Lyddite Salute', was opened by Brig O.P. Edgecumbe, CBE, MC, who said that in 1940 Lydd was at the forefront of the war and the threat of German invasion and that the bond between the military camp and the people of Lydd was magnificent. The target for the week was £15,000 to purchase five armoured cars; the final total – from Lydd, Greatstone and Dungeness – was £40,334.

During May a massive migration took place as men, machines, guns and other equipment headed for the D-Day take-off. Soldiers from many countries were brought together, but the Americans are best remembered for their generosity in handing out food and sweets. These events overshadowed a little-known tragedy that took place on the sea wall at Dymchurch on 29 May in which an officer and twenty-one men

Douglas Oiller, coxswain of the Dungeness lifeboat Charles Cooper Henderson, who with his crew rescued many friends and enemies during the war years.

were killed and several others seriously wounded. Three boxes of anti-tank grenades exploded while instruction in their use was being given to a platoon of the Somerset Regiment. An inquest was held at Dymchurch on 1 June, conducted by Coroner Maj C.F. Crabbe, with Mr J.E. Chapple as assessor. In evidence, Company Sgt Maj H.J. Smith said his men were being given instruction in anti-tank measures. Later he heard an explosion, rather too loud for one grenade. 'I saw debris in the air where they had been. I ran to the

beach. I could see a number of men had been killed and others were lying injured.'
Cpl C.E. Oxby, one of the men in the platoon, said:

Lt Wilson was giving the instruction. Sgt Hill supervised the seating on the wall steps. The boxes of grenades were on the step in front of us; the detonators were in a flat sealed tin. Lt Wilson told us we would have to throw two grenades as a prepared charge. The lids of the grenade boxes were open. He took out a grenade, removed the pressure plate, threw the plate down and put the grenade back in the box. He then cut off a bit of safety fuse 8 in long, took a detonator and, with a jack-knife, cut off the sealing wax. He showed us how to insert the fuse into the detonator and into the grenade. He then removed the fuse and detonator and put the grenade back in the box. Lt Wilson then showed us how to light the fuse the correct way. He took a box of vestas from his pocket. He took the fuse and held it in his left hand with a match. With his right hand he struck the matchbox downwards. The first match went out without lighting the fuse, so he took a second match from the box and struck it the same way. The fuse began to burn. Lt Wilson was talking to us when there was a terrific explosion.

The Coroner recorded a verdict of accidental death.

In the King's Birthday Honours on 6 June Arthur J. Gearing, MM, Chief Observer of the Dymchurch and Littlestone ROC posts, was awarded the British Empire Medal for Meritorious Service to the Royal Observer Corps. A few days after this, on 8 June, wave after wave of bombers and transport planes passed over the Marsh heading for France and fighter planes were also extremely active, patrolling the skies as well as escorting the bombers. Obviously something significant was happening. It was, of course, the day the Allies landed in Europe.

Although the war had now crossed the Channel, those who remained at home soon faced a new peril. On 12 June a rumour which had been circulating for some time became a fact – the first flying bomb arrived. With members of the Regular Army now in short supply, and the possibility of a counter invasion by the Germans, members of the Lydd, New Romney and Brenzett platoons of the Romney Marsh Home Guards were summoned to a special meeting at Lydd Drill Hall. Dave Ford, of the New Romney platoon, remembers: 'We arrived at the drill hall and noticed a sentry posted on the door. We met our officer, Tom Finn-Kelcey. He told us our commanding officer from Ashford would be coming as well as representatives from the Army and Navy. We were told that the Germans were planning to send forces to our area, because they thought the invasion into Europe was to be at Calais. We were required to – and we did – mount guard in the railway tunnel at Sandling, being taken there by Carey's bus from New Romney. We did this for about two months until the threat decreased.' Prayers were said in many of the Marsh churches for the men fighting in Normandy, and a united service at Lydd Parish Church on 18 June, conducted by the Revd Bill Britten, was attended by representatives of many branches of the armed forces.

More damaged bombers returning from Europe came down in the Marsh area in the latter half of June. In the late evening of 20 June a Liberator, with one engine in flames and another dead, crash-landed on the sands near Lade. Two of the crew baled out but their parachutes failed to open, five scrambled to safety, two more were rescued injured, and one body was recovered the following morning. On 22 June another Liberator made a forced landing on Denge beach. The crew of ten – Lts Guy Gipson, Franklin Draper, Raymond F. Pariseau, and Alvin Lichtenstein, S Sgts Donald Mann and Edward Pendowski and Sgts Richard Peters, William Stevens, Gideon Swick and Joseph Lisowski – escaped unhurt. The ten crew members of a third Liberator, crippled by enemy action on 24 June, all baled out safely between Lade and Lydd before their aircraft crashed on farmland at Jury's Gap and burned out. A fourth Liberator was seen on the 27th flying inland over New Romney with its starboard engine on fire, followed by a fifth Liberator with one engine on fire and another dead. A Lancaster bomber passed over Belgar, between New Romney and Lydd, on 29 June with both starboard engines dead and one of its wheels down. Fortunately, it landed safely at Manston.

With the Doodlebug onslaught at its height in the summer months the hard-pressed ack-ack crews became a bit 'trigger-happy'. On 4 July a Polish pilot, Stanislaw Domanski, was killed when his Tempest was accidentally brought down at East Guldeford by British gunners as he flew towards Rye having taking off from Newchurch. Two Spitfires also came under fire on the evening of 18 July as they crossed over the Marsh, but fortunately the gunners' aim was poor. Similarly, two days later thirty off-target shells greeted four Thunderbolts when they flew north over Walland Marsh. Wisely, prior warning was given to the Observer Corps, Coastguards and Police – and presumably the Army – when two British jet aircraft headed west across the Marsh at 8 p.m. on 20 July. Because of the advent of the Doodlebugs more ack-ack crews, including ATS girls, were drafted into the area, often seeing action before they had time to unpack their kit. With the guns in action for long spells day and night and their crews' tents often pitched nearby, sleep for the gunners was almost impossible.

Owing to the intensive anti-aircraft fire producing shrapnel hits on Brenzett school and its air-raid shelters, parents and pupils were asked to attend the school on 22 August (during the summer holiday) to be given information about voluntary evacuation, something not previously contemplated there even in 1940. Only four pupils chose to be evacuated. The Doodlebugs themselves posed little threat as long as they kept going towards their targets and were not hit by gunfire or shot down by aircraft. Many Marsh people now admit that they always hoped the 'damn things' would crash in somebody else's area.

Meanwhile, the enemy's long-range guns on the French coast continued to shell Folkestone and Dover, as well as any Channel convoys. In the early hours of 27 July the American steamship *Fort Perrot* sustained several hits, caught fire and was beached off Lade. The Dungeness lifeboat was launched and Coxswain Oiller later reported: 'I received the call at 3.50 a.m. I at once called out crew and launchers and we launched the boat at 4.15 a.m. and proceeded in the direction given and found a large steamer on fire. The captain said he had wounded men on board and would we take them ashore and get them to hospital at once. We landed four injured seamen at Dungeness and returned to the vessel and stood by until other assistance arrived. I then asked the captain if he required any further assistance and he replied "No". We returned to our station, arriving at 7.30 a.m.'

The coxswain's matter-of-fact report makes no mention that the sea conditions were very difficult, that there were several vessels close to shore which had to be avoided in the darkness, that boarding the *Fort Perrot* was hazardous because of the fire and that shrapnel from the ack-ack guns firing at Doodlebugs was raining down all around. In fact the lifeboat was struck three times. The *Fort Perrot* was eventually towed to Southampton.

The lifeboat helpers, many of them women, earned special mention by the lifeboat honorary secretary, Capt Quentin Crawfurd RN. He said: 'The men and women launchers dragged the lifeboat through heavy shingle with flying bombs, three at a time, passing overhead, and with the shells of the shore batteries bursting round the bombs. For four hours they worked and waited, unsheltered on this dangerous shore, while the shrapnel from the bursting shells, falling bullets and exploding bombs fell around them. They were every one of them courageous in their actions.' Coxswain Oiller and his wife had a lucky escape two days later when an ack-ack shell took off part of their bedroom roof as they slept and exploded outside, causing considerable damage.

A problem which put even Doodlebugs and shrapnel in the shade arose once the harvest began on the Marsh. Councillor A.J. Pope of Lydd accused the authorities of incompetence and fellow councillors of not addressing a very important issue. He thought it called for strong words in the right ears. The problem was an acute shortage of beer. The pubs were swamped by troops, who preferred to drink outside the camps. Councillor Pope said: 'Men are working in the fields until 8 p.m. and these workers are walking about with their tongues hanging out at night after gathering the harvest all day. We are lucky if the pubs can open two nights a week. There was more beer in 1940 than now. It's a disgrace.'

It was announced on 5 August that an acting leading Seaman, Donald Francis Jones, son of Mr and Mrs Fred Jones of Bristol House, Lydd, had been mentioned in dispatches for outstanding courage, skill and devotion to duty on successive submarine patrols. There was no relaxation of regulations ashore for three landgirls, Doris Morgan, Doreen Angus and Amy Rand, who were taken to court on 16 August by War Reserve Policeman J. Tosh at Lydd for failing to carry their identity cards. They were each fined 5s. The young people in the area were provided with entertainment when the Lydd Youth Club, with headquarters in New Lane, was officially opened. This was a farsighted move in the midst of war.

One of the biggest D-Day problems had been how to supply the Allied troops once they had landed, since the Germans had rendered the French ports almost impregnable. The solution was a floating one, made of huge, hollow, reinforced concrete blocks 70 m long, 15 m wide and 20 m high, and weighing up to 7,000 tons. More than 250 of these 'Phoenix caissons' were constructed, filled mostly with compressed air and floated across the Channel to positions just off Arromanches, Normandy, where once in place the whole structure became known as the Mulberry Harbour. Not all the caissons were required at once, so it was decided to store some at sea between Selsey and Bognor Regis and some in the East Bay, Dungeness. Army chiefs were concerned that the latter group of caissons would come under fire from the German cross-Channel guns, but the Navy replied that even if the Germans fired 1,000 rounds at them the caissons would only be hit 11 times.

A familiar sight off Littlestone today is one of the Phoenix caissons, part of the Mulberry Harbour structure used for the D-Day landings. Several caissons were stored off this part of the coast, but only this one is now visible.

This assurance was never put to the test: the Germans continued targeting Dover and presumably did not notice the activity off Dungeness.

On 31 August the Sandgate Coastguards received a request from the Army and Navy for a lifeboat to take a relief crew and provisions to Phoenix unit No. C121 anchored in East Bay. Dungeness lifeboat responded to what was a straightforward mission. However on 2 September, with the weather deteriorating, a distress call came from the same unit. Coxswain Oiller's log reads: 'At 12.45 p.m. I received a telephone message from Sandgate Coastguard station that Phoenix unit No. C121 was in difficulties again; this time she was dragging her anchor and could we go and rescue the four men aboard. I launched and proceeded in a 60 mph gale with a heavy sea running. On arriving at the casualty we took the men off under greatly difficult conditions. We returned to our station with the gale increasing and a heavy surf running, arriving at station at 3 p.m.' Incidentally, one of the great Mulberry caissons can still be seen today lying just off Littlestone.

Throughout September, as the battle of the Doodlebugs continued, it was heartening for the people of the Marsh to see waves of Liberators, Fortresses, Halifaxes, Stirlings, Dakotas, Marauders and Lightnings heading for targets on the Continent. But there was a downside: not all those aircraft returned and some that did came to grief on the verge of reaching safety.

One young American officer, a member of a bomber crew, escaped with his life, but only just, when his damaged Liberator crash-landed into a heavy sea close inshore at Greatstone, almost opposite the Jolly Fisherman, on 17 September. A young RAF doctor, Sqn Ldr D.D. Morrell, saw the bomber crash and attempted to wade out to it, but was driven back by the force of the waves and the strong current. Mr J. Frost, of the local Civil Defence unit, took control of the situation. An Army amphibious 'dukw' was commandeered to ferry Sqn Ldr Morrell to the aircraft and the other surviving crew were taken ashore. Some, however, had baled out when the aircraft was too low and had been killed when they hit the sands. The American officer was trapped in his seat by his legs and the rising tide, already up to his shoulders, threatened to drown him. Sqn Ldr Morrell repeatedly dived underwater to free him, succeeding in the nick of time; before he was taken ashore, Sqn Ldr Morrell gave him morphia because of the appalling injuries to his legs. Sqn Ldr Morrell was later awarded the OBE for his 'outstanding courage and initiative'.

On 22 September large fires could be seen and heavy explosions heard from in and around Boulogne as the Channel port was bombed by Lancasters and Halifaxes and then liberated by Canadian troops. At last the big guns that had for so long pounded Folkestone and Dover were silenced.

With less Doodlebug activity – the final one to fall on Romney Marsh landed at Lade on 5 November – and with successes by British troops in Europe bringing victory within sight, plans began to be made for the return of peace. New Romney Town Council started negotiations with the gas and electricity companies to decide whether to continue to use gas for street lighting or to switch to electricity. A demonstration was arranged and permission granted for the town's High Street to be lit for an hour by electricity; this was the first time the lamps had been switched on since 1939. It was New Romney's busiest evening of the war as members of the council were joined in their inspection by crowds of residents and scores of people who had cycled in from the surrounding area. And the verdict? Electricity.

Another sign of impending victory was the announcement on 3 December that the Kent battalions of the Home Guard could be stood down. Despite their evident shortcomings in 1940 they had developed into a formidable defence force. The year ended cold but quiet at last, with the Christmas festivities the happiest and most relaxed for six years. Church bells were rung and many lights were shown without fear of shouts of 'Put that out' or of prosecution.

FOURTEEN

THE DOODLEBUG

With the massive Allied landings in Europe on 6 June 1944, it seemed that comparative peace had at last returned to Romney Marsh. But it was not to be. Only a week later, on 13 June, Hitler launched his secret weapon, the flying bomb, and the Marsh found itself once again in the front line, with the battle to beat the robot aeroplane raging overhead.

Persistent rumours had been circulating since 1943 that the Germans were developing a pilotless plane packed with explosives, and the Royal Observer Corps, the Coastguard and the three services had been briefed about what was first code-named 'Diver', but later became known as the VI, the flying bomb, the buzz-bomb and finally – courtesy of the RAF – the Doodlebug.

It was at 4.08 a.m. on 13 June that two ROC men in their post on Martello tower No. 25 at Dymchurch saw an aircraft approaching. The late Arthur Gearing, observer in charge of the Dymchurch Group, recorded his memories of the incident in 1978:

> On duty that morning were Archie Wraight and Ern Woodland, a call from HQ in Maidstone stated that Delta 2, that was Folkestone, had reported a plane coming in on fire, and asked if we could see it. Archie Wraight focused his field-glasses on it and recognized it as a Diver. His colleague, Ern Woodland, plotted its course and rang Maidstone with the message 'Mike 2, [Dymchurch] "DIVER, DIVER, DIVER" on Four, North-West, One, O, One.' At Maidstone, as I heard later, the girl said to the supervisor, 'Mike 2 say they've got a "Diver"'. He replied 'Push it through GHQ'. At GHQ they said 'They are wrong, if a flying bomb was going to be dispatched from France we would have known'.

Even though the operations personnel were sceptical they instantly carried out the correct procedure, sounding the sirens and alerting No. 11 Fighter Group based at Uxbridge. Any doubts were soon dispelled as other ROC posts at Pluckley, Lenham and Bromley traced the machine's movements, and within 7 minutes of the Dymchurch message the Prime Minister had been told. Later Archie Wraight and Ern Woodland described the Doodlebug as 'about the size of a small fighter, on fire at the rear, and sounding like a Model-T Ford going uphill'. Gun crews spotted it as it headed inland but thought it was an aircraft, and it finally crashed near Swanscombe in Kent.

Two more Doodlebugs passed over Romney Marsh that morning: Mr Billy Cooper, the observer in the temporary ROC satellite post at Littlestone, recorded one at 4.45 a.m. and noted it in his log as having a long nose, narrow wings and a red glow 3 or 4 feet behind the wings. The third passed over Littlestone at 5 a.m. on the same route.

Ern Woodland and Archie Wraight on duty at the Observer Post atop Martello tower No. 25 at Dymchurch. It was from this tower that the two men reported sighting the first Doodlebug to reach Britain.

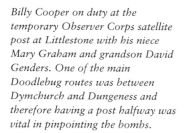

Billy Cooper on duty at the temporary Observer Corps satellite post at Littlestone with his niece Mary Graham and grandson David Genders. One of the main Doodlebug routes was between Dymchurch and Dungeness and therefore having a post halfway was vital in pinpointing the bombs.

From this time on there was a continuous stream of Doodlebugs, sometimes in excess of thirty a day, causing more alarm and wreaking more widespread havoc than the German bombers and fighters had done in earlier years. It was not just the fear of the Doodlebugs falling to the ground – although this was a constant danger – but also the tremendous barrage of shells put up by our guns as soon as one appeared. It was deafening night and day, and extremely frightening for the old and very young, with shrapnel raining down and shells damaging roofs of houses as the elevation of the guns lowered, for many Doodlebugs flew below 1,000 ft and, once hit, even lower. Those which escaped the coastal guns were then pursued by fighter planes, which destroyed many before they reached the bordering hills.

Romney Marsh was still, without doubt, a perilous place in which to live during the summer months of 1944. The schoolchildren who chose to remain in the area spent most of their school hours in the air-raid shelters. Brenzett had no air-raid siren, although if the weather conditions were right, the New Romney or Lydd ones could be heard there. Therefore, a senior pupil was put on duty in the playground during breaks, with a tin hat and a whistle, and at any sight or sound of aircraft he blew the whistle and all the pupils went to the shelters.

A pursuing Typhoon successfully 'wing-tips' a Doodlebug above farmland between Lydd and New Romney. This method of bringing them down was discouraged by the RAF, *who preferred pilots to use their guns from a safe distance. Drawn by Malcolm Timms.*

The first of the Doodlebugs came from launching bases situated between Dunkirk and Rouen and were generally sighted in Britain between Dymchurch and Beachy Head. Because of their straight flight-path, unless they were hindered in any way they passed on to targets further inland and were therefore of no danger to the coastal population. But when hit, they became entirely unpredictable, sometimes falling or gliding to earth, but more often than not performing the sort of aerobatics a display team would be proud of. Once down, however, the warhead caused an immense amount of damage. Diaries, official records and personal memories tell of the large numbers of Doodlebugs that passed over and speak of those that crashed in Romney Marsh and the surrounding countryside. The rest of Kent and Sussex and Essex also bore their share of tragedy and destruction as a result of these devices.

Just how many Doodlebugs passed over and how many crashed and where is uncertain. Even the official figures for Romney Marsh are contradictory. The most reliable records are those in the logbooks of the ROC and the Coastguard. From these sources it is known that from 13 June to 2 September Doodlebugs were a daily menace. One of five ROC points recorded more than 180 in June, 550 in July, 420 in August and 3 in September. The last two seen and heard were, appropriately, on 5 November, one coming down on Denge Beach and the other crashing into the hillside at Winchelsea.

The earliest Doodlebugs were fairly easy to plot but the gun batteries at that time consisted mainly of Bofors guns, which had very limited success in stopping them. Ben

Tart of the ROC post at Dungeness saw the limitations of these guns: 'When the Doodlebugs started, the ones that came into our area came between Dymchurch and Dungeness. They came over our post, and it was rare at that time for them to fly further west, they flew a set course. The first few weeks were the worst; all we had were Bofors guns, which were not much good. I've stood and watched Bofors shells hit and bounce off again. Therefore, it was largely left to the RAF fighters to deal with these bombs. Sterling work was carried out by squadrons from Newchurch and Brenzett advance landing grounds. Many of the gun crews shared Ben Tart's frustration but kept trying, causing more damage, perhaps, than the Doodlebugs.

As the number of Doodlebugs increased, urgent steps were taken to move heavy ack-ack batteries to the south coast, manned by mixed crews and assisted by radar units with the new rocket-firing Z batteries, which sent up a barrage of rockets and were very noisy if you were close to them. The gun sites used the GPO network for communication purposes, and Edward Ralph, a young apprentice to engineer Jack Bayley, remembers visiting gun positions to service and restore cables. 'Most of the gun sites had their telephone cables at the top of our poles and above our cables. We would sometimes be up a pole when a Doodlebug was spotted. The sound from the guns was terrific and when these rockets arrived they were in something like a dustbin, and when fired they all went up together making a tremendous sound. They were, I gather, very successful against the Doodlebug.'

Another member of the local services who had to make frequent calls on the gun sites was George Warren from Dymchurch, who was a repairman for the Folkestone Electricity Company. He remembers visiting a gun site near Brookland: 'Just after I arrived a Doodlebug came over fairly close to us, and the neighbouring guns opened fire while this gun crew took shelter. Afterwards I asked them why they had not opened fire as they were closer than some. The sergeant told me it had been a busy morning with many Doodlebugs and they were now out of ammunition. This apparently happened often.'

Mrs P. Frost, a member of the ATS serving with a mixed heavy ack-ack battery, recollects being posted to Romney Marsh:

When I arrived at Camber in the summer of 1944 we were put in a field under canvas. Ridge tents they were called. This site had once been a holiday camp of some sort, as there was this large building which had been used as an entertainment hall; this became the cookhouse and battery office. The tents were rather small for four girls sharing, and that summer was a rather wet one, and to touch the inside of the tent induced the rainwater to come in, so everything got rather damp.

Perhaps I was more lucky than most, for I had friends in nearby Lydd, Mr and Mrs George Coleman and their daughters Rosemary and Pat. So when I could, I would cycle to Lydd on the battery bike for a much-needed bath and hair wash. It was essential to wear your tin hat on the way, because, when the guns along that road opened up, there was great danger from the falling shrapnel. The usual procedure was to jump in the nearest dip until the firing ceased.

It was wonderful to be able to have a proper bath, for we had so little water in camp. What we did have came from Lydd in a fire tender, and we were each allowed one bowlful per day, cold of course. The first thing to do was to take out a mugful to clean

Guns of the US Army brought down to the coast at Littlestone to help combat the Doodlebugs.

your teeth, then wash your knife, fork and spoon, these having been given a preliminary wash in a tub of dirty water at the cookhouse. Then you washed yourself, and finally the water was used for washing stockings or smalls.

There were, of course, many guns at Camber and also along the coast in both directions. In front of us were the RAF regiment with their Bofors guns, we having heavy ack-ack 3.7 in guns, and behind us was the fighter belt. Each battery had its own arc to fire in, you were not allowed to fire outside that. Sometimes the fighters would come in pursuit of a Doodlebug where you were firing, and there was nothing much you could do. We couldn't cease fire until we were given the order. Luckily we never hit any.

The American forces played an important part in the defence against the Doodlebug, and in July 1944 the 125th Anti-Aircraft Gun Battalion moved into Romney Marsh. One member of the battalion was nineteen-year-old Charles Carome, and on a recent visit to this area he kindly recorded his memories of this period:

We arrived in Kent on 21 July 1944; our headquarters were in a summer camp on Romney Marsh. A and B batteries were on the Littlestone Golf Course at New Romney, C battery was at Dymchurch and D was at Hythe. On Saturday 22 July B battery completed setting up the guns and range-finding equipment, but we had no ammunition. Our battery commander, Capt Joseph Adderley, held a meeting to tell us that we were located on a famous golf course, now a sheep pasture. Our mission was to help in shooting down flying bombs. In addition to the newest models of range-finding

An American radar tracker crew at Littlestone, 1944. Radar was a vital piece of equipment in the fight against the Doodlebugs.

equipment, we would have a secret weapon, a new fuse for the ammunition. We saw several flying bombs, or rather we caught glimpses of small airplanes with fire shooting from their tail as they scooted through the clouds.

The gun crews finally brought in a truck-load of 90 millimetre ammunition from a supply depot during the night. Sgt Kable, chief of the range section, assigned my friend Herb and me to the new M-2 tracker which transmitted data to the range-finding computer. He showed us how to find a target in its two telescopes and how to keep the target centered in the scope cross-hairs. With those brief instructions, we were ready.

That night we watched the long flashes of British 3.7 in heavy guns and long lines of tracer flashes from lighter 40 mm Bofors guns and 20 mm cannon. Now and then we saw a British rocket battery send up a solid pattern of bursts. I wrote a letter home to tell my family that we had seen flying bombs. We were not allowed to say where we were or what we were doing in England.

The next morning our first target almost got us when the other crew fired at 5 a.m. Those of us sleeping in the tents woke up as the guns went off. We heard excited shouts and the ground shook from a heavy explosion. The target blew up about 300 yd in front of the battery.

On the following day our off-duty living arrangements took a definite turn for the better when we moved into Marlborough House, a small, old hotel at Littlestone-on-Sea which was 2 miles away by truck or less than a mile and a half if we walked through the open fields. Marlborough House was part of a solid block of hotels that faced the sea. A British 20 mm battery had its guns emplaced at the edge of the sea wall opposite our front door, and a 40 mm battery was set up nearby.

Early on the second morning at the hotel there was a VI attack. One bomb came in low over the water, it was headed straight for several of us where we stood in the doorway. The British gunner on a 20 mm cannon a few yards away hit it, and the target blew up in the air. He saved his own life and ours. When danger was apparent it was too late to run for cover.

After a few days we began to fortify our battery position. Because of the high water table we could dig pits only 2 ft deep. Then we had to construct sandbag walls around each piece of equipment. We brought in truckloads of sand from the beach and became experts in sandbagging. The largest piece of equipment was the radar. It was housed in a large closed trailer of the type used to haul goods on our highways today. Nevertheless, we managed to stack sandbags as high as its roof.

Sandbagging continued through most of August. We built shelters for each crew on duty with curved steel sections of Nissen huts brought from an abandoned airfield. Our range-tracker pit had grass sods on top of the bags to keep sand from the delicate scopes and from blowing into our eyes.

Of course our main job was firing at flying bombs, which came in almost every day and night. The first warning was telephoned from Ack-Ack OR (Anti-aircraft Operations Room) as soon as targets were spotted by 'master radars' on the coast. Our radar immediately began to search the sector where Ack-Ack OR said they could find it. At the range-tracker we watched the area close to the horizon – too low for stars to be seen. On a clear night a 'star' would appear, and we could see it moving in the tracker scopes. The flame from the VI's jet engine was visible in the scopes up to 17 miles away. Eventually, our radar was able to pick up targets before they left the coast of France.

With radar and the visual tracker on the target, data would begin flowing to the computer. When the data 'settled down', the battery was ready to fire. Maximum range

US Army B Battery, Littlestone, 1944. Two of the four guns are in firing position; the gun crews' tents can be seen in the foreground on the right.

for 90 mm guns was about 12,000 yd (6.8 miles). When the officer commanded 'Commence firing', the four gun crews would load and shoot as rapidly as possible, up to sixteen rounds per minute. In our area there might be four other batteries firing on the same target. After a few seconds, projectiles would begin to burst around the bomb. If the VI exploded in the air it was a Category A hit ('Cat A'); if it crashed on the ground it was Category B. The battery recorded range and direction data where the VI exploded, then telephoned Ack-Ack OR to register a claim on the target.

Conditions were not always ideal for most effective firing. Because VIs flew low, radar had problems with echoes from the ground. About mid-August Dr Lovell visited the battery. I don't know if he was British or American, but he was said to have developed the SCR-584 radar. [Dr A.C.B. Lovell, British radar pioneer, later Sir Bernard Lovell.] He tuned our radar (and others in the area); from then on it was 'red hot' and able to pick up targets at maximum range.

Flying bombs came in two and three at a time. The most intense action occurred when a target approached directly overhead. Afterwards shrapnel – jagged pieces of steel from the burst artillery projectiles – would drop into the battery area. Strangely enough, only one man was ever struck, and he had only a minor cut on his face.

Certain events stand out in the weeks of flying bomb action:

August 6. A VI came down on the gravel beach directly in front of Pope's Hotel. The explosion made a hole only a few inches deep, but it smashed the roof of that nice hotel.

August 15. We fired on an American fighter plane. In the tracker scope in late afternoon, the sun's reflection on its white nose looked like an engine flame. Its outline and straight course were also typical for a VI, so I made a positive identification, and we fired. The projectile bursts were just beginning to centre on the target when it suddenly zoomed straight up out of the line of fire. I immediately yelled, 'It's a plane!' The pilot reacted very quickly, and we didn't think that he was hit. The airplane appeared to be a P-47 Thunderbolt fighter-bomber. The radar crew said later that the airplane's flight pattern made it look like a VI on their scope too. He was in a 'no aircraft' area and probably was not one of the airplanes on anti-robot duty.

August 24. In the evening we were firing and tracking by radar a target that we could not see through the mist. We could tell from the sound of the projectile bursts that the range was closing rapidly. Suddenly I saw a VI out in front of the battery. There was no engine sound; it seemed to be just sitting in the air, only wobbling a little. I heard the men in the cook tent running toward a ditch across the highway, and I started to climb out of the pit to join them. However, the sergeant with us stayed cool and ordered, 'Get down!' A slight breeze finally made the target loop to the north. We heard a crash and saw a cloud of smoke over Battery A of the 124th Battalion on the beach a mile away. It looked like a direct hit, and some of our men rushed down there in two trucks. However, the VI had cleared their positions fairly well. Two men were injured, not seriously, and Battery A fired at the next target half an hour later.

During those eventful weeks, there was some social life when we were off duty. It didn't take long for us to discover that British 3.7 in battery range equipment was operated by women of the Auxiliary Territorial Service (ATS). We also met them as

US guns in action at night during a Doodlebug assault, 1944.

vehicle drivers, and they were the voices on the Ack-Ack OR telephone. There was opportunity for social contact at local pubs, and a few B Battery men had ATS girl friends. Headquarters Battery organized a dance band with the Royal Artillery. Dances were held frequently and were well attended by people off duty.

A week after the VI attacks ended we began to tear down sandbags and to return the sand to the beach.

On September 13 the battalion dressed in its best uniforms and marched to a review area on the golf course. Many British and American units were there. General Sir Frederick Pile, chief of British Anti-aircraft Artillery, addressed the group. We gave him a cheer, and he recounted the history of the flying bomb. He said we had been in the first battle in a new type of warfare with robot weapons. Anti-aircraft effectiveness had increased from 17 per cent of targets destroyed in mid-June to 74 per cent shot down in the last week of August.

During six weeks of flying bomb action in England, B Battery engaged 279 VIs and claimed 73 destroyed with 8,500 artillery rounds expended. We were an efficient unit at New Romney, and we were proud of our record there.

No Marsh town or village escaped damage from the Doodlebugs, or from the guns and planes seeking to destroy them. Sadly, there were civilian as well as service fatalities, and many suffered injuries but the numbers were low considering the widespread damage. One of the first incidents took place on 23 June 1944 when a Doodlebug was hit by a fighter plane over Brenzett and came down at Snargate, close to Hope Cottages. Joyce Bates, née Newton, remembers:

I was almost eleven years old at the time. We were all in bed; it was 3 a.m – I know that because all the clocks stopped. It was a good job we were in bed, for perhaps I wouldn't be here today. The Doodlebug dropped about 200 yd down in the field from our house. Apparently, it had glided along from Brenzett, so we did not hear it coming. The Brenzett ARP men followed it along on their cycles, so they reached us quite quickly. It demolished the side of our cottage, which bore the brunt of the explosion. One wall of my bedroom was wooden, as part of the stairway. This fell across my bed, luckily saving me. I was covered in bricks, plaster, wood, tiles and glass. First thing I remember was being tunnelled in; I couldn't move and it was terribly hot by my head. I was told afterwards that part of the Doodlebug was lying on my pillow, it was fortunate the hot metal didn't catch the bedclothes alight. I heard my Mum and Dad in the next room calling out to me, telling me to stay down. I couldn't move anyway! My Father started knotting the sheets to get at the window as there were no stairs now. My Mum called out for help and my Father said: 'Can't you shout louder?' The ARP men said later they could hear her as they came from Brenzett; we had been deafened by the explosion, so that our hearing was impaired.

Mr Harold Body and his housekeeper Miss Rose from the nearby Hope Farm arrived with a ladder, and they got my Mum and Dad down. By this time the ARP men had arrived and my schoolmaster, Mr Evans, came up the ladder and rescued me. Mrs Body took us to my grandmother's at Brattle House, Brookland. As we were leaving I said to my Mum: 'Have you locked the door?' It sounds stupid now, for all the doors and windows were missing, but I suppose I was still in shock. Apart from suffering from deafness we were unhurt. Our next-door neighbours, Mr and Mrs Frost, were still up and, as their windows came in, they were slightly cut by the flying glass.

George Elvy, a looker tending his sheep at Midley, recalls the occurrence when a Doodlebug fell on an Army camp site on 26 July 1944: 'I was told this day to remove all sheep from a field at Old Cheyne Court because the Army wanted it for a camp site. Three soldiers arrived and started putting up dozens of tents as 300 mixed Army personnel were arriving, as well as their large guns, the next day. Early that morning a Doodlebug dropped into that field, killing two of the soldiers as they slept. The other soldier, who was further over in the field, was injured but survived. Later that day soldiers and ATS girls arrived. It doesn't bear thinking about what could have happened.'

On 28 July a Doodlebug, hit by ack-ack fire, came down at Camber, demolishing the church, the school and the village hall. Several houses, as well as the post office, were badly damaged. Two men had a lucky escape on 6 August, for at 6.03 a.m., Billy Cooper was on duty at the ROC satellite post at Littlestone and observed a Doodlebug coming in at wave height directly towards him. He dashed out to the coastguard lookout next door, alerted the man on duty and they both dived down the bank. The Doodlebug crashed on to the beach in front of the two lookouts' posts, demolishing both of them. The two men

The barn at Granary Corner, Lydd, was completely destroyed by a Doodlebug that fell on 29 August 1944. The surrounding houses were also badly damaged.

were unhurt and the ROC post was operating again within a few hours, rebuilt by the Dymchurch men themselves. A plaque has recently been placed near this site at Littlestone to commemorate the little-known work of the ROC during this period.

On the afternoon of 15 August another Doodlebug hit by guns came down in Dymchurch recreation ground. A young baby, Eric Newman, was killed and his father, Jack Newman, and two young girls, Daphne Austin and Jean Ovenden, were seriously injured. A few weeks later on 29 August, just after 11 a.m., a Doodlebug hit by ack-ack guns exploded on top of a barn at Granary Corner, Lydd (now reconstructed as Lydd Youth Club). It is thought it hit the kingpost, some 20 ft above the ground, which is why it caused so much devastation in the town. As well as the barn, 3 houses were demolished, including the public house First and Last, 16 were seriously damaged, 20 had major damage and 250 suffered some damage. Also 1 person was fatally injured, 2 others seriously injured and 15 slightly hurt. Thanks to an early warning, most people had taken to their air-raid shelters.

Doreen Allen, née Godfrey, a young teenager at the time, remembers coming home and seeing all the damage in her street. 'A Mrs Drake, née Prebble, from the First and Last, told me my mother was hurt. Well, I just ran towards home. A policeman tried to stop me because of the live electric wires on the ground, but I dodged round him and kept going. What had happened was the roof of the shelter had been blown off, and that hit my mother's shoulder. Our home had lost the roof, doors and windows. Mrs Claude Paine, of the WVS, took us all to The Lodge in Dennes Lane, where we were given a meal. In the meantime our home was patched up. Everybody then was so helpful and kind.'

Jack Flisher, a farmworker, had turned Granary Corner only a few minutes before the incident happened:

I passed by on a tractor, and when I got further along, almost to the station bridge, I heard the explosion over the noise of the nearby guns which were firing. I looked back and could see little for smoke and dust. Well, my wife and two young sons lived a few yards up from the corner. I left the tractor and ran back. Why I didn't go on the tractor I don't know, as it would have been quicker. All I was worried about was what I might find, as things looked bad. The whole corner had gone, rubble was everywhere, and the air was still thick with dust. I arrived at Grisbrook Cottage where we lived, the doors were off, the windows were in, and half the roof had been torn off. I went indoors, there were the saucepans still cooking on the stove. I shouted and called, but there was no sign of anyone, I really was worried. Then Mrs Inder, who lived next door and was also an ARP warden, told me she had taken them in and they were okay.

But I couldn't believe her until I saw them. My wife had taken shelter under the big old kitchen table. Only my youngest son Derrick had a few scratches on his arms. They were lucky.

All three services helped overcome the Doodlebug, as did many civilian organizations, but the one recognized by the authorities as playing a major role was the Royal Observer Corps, responsible for sighting and plotting the course of the robot planes. Among the observers were those at Dymchurch, Dungeness and Brookland, their colleagues just off the Marsh at Lyminge, Ham Street and Rye Harbour, and at the satellite post at Littlestone, manned by the Dymchurch ROC. Bob Gearing, son of Arthur Gearing, head of the Dymchurch post, used to accompany his father to the ROC post, even later on when he was on leave from the RAF. He recalls:

Archie Wraight and Arthur Gearing in the Observer Corps post on Martello tower No. 24 at Dymchurch, 1939.

The original post was on Tower 24, in the village itself. The ROC shared this with the coastguard, two machine-guns posts and an artillery observer. As you can imagine it was rather crowded, so in 1941 the ROC moved to Tower 25, which was reinforced for the purpose and a post built on the top. In 1943 a satellite post was built at Littlestone in preparation for Hitler's secret weapon, the Doodlebug.

To draw the attention of our patrolling fighters to the presence of a Doodlebug, the observer would fire a parachute rocket. These would be plugged into an electric socket to set them off, and a fighter pilot would know that a Doodlebug would be within half a mile of a flare. I used to come home on leave and go to the post, and the Doodlebugs would be coming in and everything

Even today parts of Doodlebugs can be found on Denge Beach, such as this section of the impulse duct.

Part of the fuselage of a Doodlebug brought down near the Denge Beach water tower on 23 August 1944.

would be going up at them. From Dymchurch through to the west were battery after battery of guns, and just back from the coast there were more guns, and the shells from these would be going over you. It was like hell let loose; the noise of the rockets and guns was absolutely deafening. Any Doodlebug which got through faced the waiting Tempests and Spitfires, and after that there were the barrage balloons to be contended with.

Even though the Doodlebugs had all but ceased by September, until the end of the war in Europe the ROC stations kept a watchful eye on all aircraft coming or going across the Channel. On VE Day, 8 May 1945, a message was received from the group commandant ROC and all officers of No. 1 Group: 'We could not let this important day pass without expressing our sincere appreciation of all you have done to help in this great achievement. It is hoped in the near future to pass to you stand-down orders, and until that day arrives we are certain that you will carry out the duties entrusted to you realizing that the final days of vigilance may be the means of saving further lives.' The stand-down came four days later at 12.02 p.m. on 12 May. Although the Doodlebugs were active for only eighty days, it affected so many lives that it is the time most people recall when they discuss Romney Marsh at war.

FIFTEEN

1945

The end of hostilities came in 1945. But before the rejoicing could begin in Romney Marsh there was a bitter January to endure, an accident which claimed the lives of four young soldiers and two final sea dramas.

By 7 January the temperature had dropped to 21°F, with heavy falls of snow driven by gale-force winds blocking most of the Marsh roads. The sea was iced over along the edge of the beach and at Dungeness the milk froze as it was delivered. Another gale began on 13 January and brought yet more drifts, defeating the efforts of those trying to keep the railways and roads clear. Although the winds eventually moderated, temperatures remained

The welfare officers for East Kent. Miss Anne Roper, on the left, was responsible for Romney Marsh. All service personnel came under her wing, and in particular the three women's services and the landgirls. She was awarded the MBE in 1945.

below freezing until 3 February. A spell of exceptionally warm, still weather followed which created mirages at sea. Several times the rescue services were called out to investigate what turned out to be nothing more than flotsam.

Two Marsh personalities had received the MBE in the New Year's Honours List. The first was Miss Anne Roper for her work as a welfare officer to the Women's Land Army, the ATS and the WAAF and for arranging entertainment for service personnel in the area. The second was the Mayor of Lydd, Alderman G.T. Paine, for his work in Civil Defence and as head of the War Agriculture Committee for the Marsh.

Preparations for peace were getting underway and on 1 March work began on clearing minefields and demolishing blockhouses in the centre of towns. Many coastal defences were removed, giving the public access to the shore once more. But Dungeness remained a restricted area because of the PLUTO operation.

An inquest held on 13 March heard how four young soldiers stationed at Lydd Camp were killed when a 2-in mortar exploded as it was being fired. Maj John Richard Allen, Royal Army Ordnance Corps, senior investigation officer for Eastern Command, said he had no theories to explain what might have happened. A verdict of accidental death was recorded.

The final war drama at sea in which the Dungeness lifeboat was involved took place on 9 April when Coxswain Doug Oiller heard two heavy explosions and a ship sounding SOS on its siren. He said: 'I launched the lifeboat at 9.40 p.m. Proceeding to the scene of the casualty I found a steamer which had been torpedoed in the stern. I went on board at the captain's request and he told me he had one man blown overboard, one seriously injured, one slightly injured. I offered to take the injured ashore but one was too ill to move. The captain asked me if I could search for the missing seaman, which I agreed to do. We searched without success. We returned to our station at 12.20 a.m.' This steamer, *Solomon Juneau*, an American ship travelling in convoy, was one of several damaged in the Channel that evening by U-boats. After the war it was revealed that U-boats, including the midget type, had been very active during this period between Folkestone and Dungeness.

On 20 April all blackout restrictions were lifted and street lighting restored. It was also announced at Romney Marsh sessions that no cases of drunkenness had been reported in the past year, and that during the war years generally cases had been surprisingly low considering the large number of servicemen in the area.

With the strings of Allied successes being reported daily on the wireless and in the newspapers, it came as no great surprise, but as an immense relief, when on 8 May Winston Churchill announced to the nation that the war with Germany was over and that 9 May would be a public holiday. As the air-raid sirens in Lydd sounded a celebratory last 'all clear', one old gentleman mistook it for a warning and dashed down into the public shelter in the High Street, only emerging after some persuasion.

The Marsh greeted VE Day with flying flags, services of thanksgiving and, a little later, fun days for the young and not-so-young. In gaily decorated Lydd two services were conducted by the Revd William Britton in the war-damaged and patched-up parish church of All Saints and attended by the mayor and members of the corporation. In the evening Lydd Camp hosted a dance, relaying the music of the military band into the town by means of loudspeakers, along with a message from the officers and men wishing the people of Lydd all happiness in the days to come.

Men and women of Dymchurch who served during the war are honoured at a dinner held for them by the Dymchurch British Legion, 1946.

In New Romney at a thanksgiving service in the parish church of St Nicholas, the mayor, Alderman Cavey addressed a large congregation:

At last, after nearly six years, the war with Germany is at an end. The Germans have been beaten very decisively and our grateful thanks are due to the men and women of the services; to our allies; to those people who have produced the weapons; and, of course, to our Lord Warden, Mr Churchill. I feel this occasion is one more for thanksgiving than for celebration, for there is no doubt that we in this borough have great reason to be thankful when we remember the great number of bombs and flying bombs that fell around us. Not one fell in the town itself, but it may interest you to know that in this area we endured 174 incidents, 720 high-explosive bombs, approximately 2,823 incendiaries, 150 flying bombs and 38 crashed aircraft.

May God grant that our forces be successful against Japan in the very near future.

Then came the fun with parties, sports, jellies, trifles and cakes.

First to celebrate by holding a party and sports day was New Romney on 18 May in the church hall and the adjacent field, colourfully decorated by members of the Civil Defence. Sports and games were organized by Mr Humphreys, prizes were given by the WVS, and a tea party was provided by the town council, to music by Mr Arthur Ashdown's barrel organ, followed by Mr Frank Peters' Punch and Judy show.

Lydd firemen at the Victory Parade, 1945. Left to right: R. Wellstead, S. Boulden, F. Austin, J. Munds, W. Webb, T. Else, B. Browning, E. Frampton, P. Olver.

On 21 May 200 children of Dymchurch and district marched to the recreation ground, led by a pipe major of the Royal Artillery, and then took part in sports for all ages organized by Sgt Maj Champion. Afterwards everyone went back to the village for a jelly and cream cake feast arranged by Mr and Mrs R.W. Andrew and helpers. Following entertainment by Messrs Goodwin and Harris, more than forty sports prizes were handed out by Mrs Andrew and as the young guests departed for home each was given 4s to be spent on the purchase of savings stamps. A special gift was posted to Daphne Austin, who was still recovering from the injuries she had received when a Doodlebug fell on the village.

On the same day 300 Lydd children, as well as their parents and servicemen from the military camp, took part in sports on the Rype. Sack, wheel, threadneedle, backstay, three-legged and egg-and-spoon races caused great amusement, especially when the grown-ups had a go. Tea followed in the Guildhall and the Salvation Army Hut in New Street, with members of Lydd Youth Club serving the sandwiches, jelly, trifle and cakes. A letter was read out from Queen Wilhelmina of the Netherlands thanking the youth club for raising money for the distressed children of her country. In the evening there was more entertainment on the Rype and as dusk fell, games and dances continued in the Institute.

A sunny 7 July saw the turn of St Mary-in-the-Marsh to celebrate. More than 100 children and adults gathered in a gaily decorated meadow, loaned by Mr T. Boyd of Haffenden Farm, and played games, competed in races and then enjoyed a delicious tea. In addition to sports prizes, each child up to the age of fourteen received a sixpence.

On 15 July, young mother Mrs R. Graham-Brown was walking along Dymchurch sea wall with her 22-month-old daughter when two members of a party of soldiers sunbathing on the steep face of the wall were washed into the sea by a big wave. One scrambled back to safety

BOROUGH OF LYDD LOCAL SAVINGS COMMITTEE

Chairman: Alderman G. T. PAINE, Mayor of Lydd

VICTORY & THANKS-SAVINGS WEEK

Saturday, September 22nd to Saturday, September 29th (inclusive)

Hon. Secretary:	*Hon. Treasurer:*	*Campaign H.Q.:*
Mr. D. C. NICOL, M.S.I.A.	Mrs. WELLSTEAD	TOWN HALL,
		LYDD, KENT

TO THE PEOPLE OF LYDD, DUNGENESS & GREATSTONE.

A little more than a year ago, we held our Salute the Soldier Week. By investing £40,334, and winning the Flag for Small Savings for the whole of Kent, Lydd, Dungeness and Greatstone did splendidly. It was an exciting coincidence that on the last day of our Salute the Soldier Week, Rome fell to the United Nations, and on the very next day, our boys landed in Normandy.

So much has happened since—the Flying Bombs and Rockets, the Fall of Paris, Arnhem, Crossing the Rhine, the German unconditional surrender, the atomic bomb, the unconditional surrender of Japan and . . . PEACE. Tremendous events which must surely arouse in us the overwhelming desire to give Thanks. Our first thoughts, perhaps, are of a job magnificently done—by our fighting men, by the Home Guard and Civil Defence, by the men and women on the land and in the factories, by our housewives and by the entire nation roused to its greatest and most intense pitch of accomplishment. In that all-out effort, the Savings Movement has played a worthy part.

Are we, after all these long years of War to go on Saving, to go on denying ourselves the things we have been so much looking forward to having? The answer is an emphatic " **YES** "—for it is the only answer which can hold the promise of a happier and more prosperous Britain. All through the War we have been saving for the purpose of destruction. Our own survival was at stake and we could do no other. But now we are urged to save for the purpose of construction—for all the nobler and finer and most civilising things of this world.

Our victory and Thanks-Savings Week will start by a Grand Victory Parade, led by the Band of the Royal West Kent Regiment, and representative of the Forces and I hope also of all organisations and sections of the Community which have taken part in the struggle at Home. The Parade, after a short march through the Town, will form up for the Official Opening of the Week by the Lord Lieutenant of Kent, Lord Cornwallis, K.B.E., M.C. A full programme is being arranged for the Week, including a Torch-Light Procession, Community Singing around the Bon-Fire, Grand Dances and Whist Drives, Special Films to be shown by the mobile cinema, exhibitions, a Garden Fete (with side-shows, baby show and children's fancy dress), etc., full details of which will be announced later. All proceeds from the social events of the Week will be handed to the Town's Fund for Commemorating the sacrifice, the noble endeavour and the high purpose of the past six years.

Our War Savings Campaigns have resulted as follows: Warships Week—£29,189 (including New Romney and Romney Marsh). Wings for Victory Week—£32,230 (Lydd's first big Week on its own). Salute the Soldier Week—£40,334 (and we won the County Flag for Small Savings).

We must make our Victory and Thanks-Savings Week the greatest Week of all, for it is a salute to **all** the Fighting Services, to all men and women who have taken part in the struggle at home, and a Salute to the Youth and the Future Citizens of our Country.

May we beat all previous records and show that we are just as determined to play our part in the Peace for which so much was sacrificed in the War.

8th September, 1945.   GORDON T. PAINE.

A pamphlet promoting 'Victory and Thanks-Savings Week' at Lydd, Dungeness and Greatstone.

but the other was swept backwards and forwards in deep water. None of his comrades could swim, so the lady sprang into action. Handing her young daughter to a nearby paratrooper, she dived into the water fully clothed and succeeded, after a prolonged effort, in pushing the drowning soldier up against the wall. As he was pulled out she herself got into difficulties but some of the soldiers tied several towels together to form a rope which she was able to grasp and be lifted out of the sea. Quickly retrieving her daughter, she went off to change without giving her name and address, but was later traced and received a bravery award.

New Romney – which at the time had a population of about 2,000 – had more than its share of brave men. In five years of war they gained 1 VC, 2 DSOs, 1 DFC, 1 DSM, 4 MCs, 1 OBE, 1 MBE, and 3 Mentions in Dispatches. On 7 August it was reported that Lydd had scored another wartime achievement. Already the holder of the county championship flag for War Savings, its Red Cross Penny-a-Week Fund, which had just closed, had collected £1,243 16s 3d, the highest total in Kent on a penny per person per week basis.

Lydd's 'Victory Queen' Jean Sims with her attendants Hilary Brattle and Doris Stickells tour the town, 22 September 1945.

Seven days later, on 14 August, came the second great bit of news of the war. Prime Minister Clement Attlee announced to the nation the surrender of Japan – and declared the next day a public holiday. Opening Lydd's Victory and Thanksgiving Week on 22 September, Lord Cornwallis, KCB, MC, Lord Lieutenant of Kent paid tribute to the people of Romney Marsh. A large procession toured the town led by the Band of the Royal West Kents.

In his address to the large crowd, Lord Cornwallis asked the people to be joyous in victory and sincere in thanksgiving, adding:

We have been fighting for freedom and liberty and also for our lives. Do you remember the evacuation of the sheep and children? Do you remember when I had to tell you that some of you here probably would never get back over the Royal Military Canal? Do you remember that Romney Marsh was very nearly flooded as a last attempt to stop what we thought was an absolutely certain invasion at that moment? There was no person here at that time whose life was not in peril.

You have seen the war, you took part in the battle, you have braved the dangers of war. You remember the 'Few'; you saw them. You recollect the flying bomb; your ears were deafened by the din of the anti-aircraft batteries. There are many parts of this small island of England which did not even know there was a war on. You set an example that kept up the national morale.

Someone may say to you one day: 'Where were you in the Second World War?' And you can say: 'I was in Romney Marsh.'

INDEX